Social Anthropology

FRANK KERMODE, General Editor

Ethology, Robert A. Hinde
Religion, Leszek Kolakowski
Social Anthropology, Edmund Leach

Social Anthropology

Edmund Leach

New York   Oxford
OXFORD UNIVERSITY PRESS
1982

Copyright © 1982 by Edmund Leach

Paperback edition published in Great Britain by Fontana Paperbacks, 1982

Library of Congress Catalog Card Number: 81-85134

Printing (last digit): 9 8 7 6 5 4 3 2 1

Printed in the United States of America

Contents

Introduction

This brief Introduction is intended to provide some guidelines for my potential readers. The book is not a textbook for undergraduates; it does not provide any stock answers to examination questions for those who have not done their serious reading beforehand, though maybe some undergraduate students of social anthropology who already know more or less what they are up to might turn in better essays and term papers than they do if they first fully understood what I have to say.

Nor is my book addressed to professional anthropological colleagues most of whom are likely to be contemptuous of the style of anthropology which it advocates and which they may well denounce as old-fashioned, egocentric, unscientific, escapist, lacking in coherence, political commitment, and so on. If I had to write a review of the book I would probably say something of this sort myself but most of these deficiencies are intentional.

I set out to write about the kind of social anthropology which I myself find interesting and to which from time to time I have made a contribution. That meant looking at the subject from an egocentric and historical point of view. My educational background was in mathematics and engineering; my initial adult experience was in commerce; but in 1937 I was 'converted' to social anthropology and, apart from the frustrations of military service between 1939 and 1946, the theory and practice of social anthropology has been a personal obsession ever since.

In the early days, my interests, like those of my contemporaries and immediate seniors in the profession, lay mainly in kinship and social organization. These 'classical' fields of anthropological enquiry may not seem very close to the area to which I now devote most of my professional attention which may be described, very roughly, as the interface between art and religious ideology. But, in my own case, the latter interests grew out of the former. Moreover, in so far as I have a utilizable 'theory' which is applicable to the study of art and mythology and religious rituals, it is a theory which developed from the fact that at the time when I conducted my first anthropological fieldwork (among the Yami of Botel Tobago in 1936), I had the competences of an engineer but not those of an anthropologist.

There is very little about art and religion in this book because what I might like to say on these matters tends to become hopelessly distorted if it is compressed. But the theory is there. It is a very simple theory which is very widely employed in many branches of mathematics. It can be summarized by saying that the relationship between the three symbols '+', '−' and '0' can best be shown as a triangle:

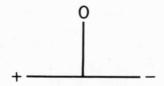

'+/−' form a binary pair, they are 'equal and opposite' in every respect but also inseparable, since neither can be understood without cognizance of the other. But '0' is not only 'in the middle', 'betwixt and between'; it is of a different kind. And yet, if one moved along an imaginary continuous path containing, as points, all the numbers between '+1' and '−1', one would necessarily pass through a point marked '0', which is neither '+' nor '−' but both at once.

I am sorry to start off with such an alarmingly abstract formulation but the problem which underlies it is extremely general and of very fundamental importance to all of us. How do the discontinuities of time and space which we seem to recognize at one level tie in with the continuities which we experience at another?

Human beings of every kind, in every kind of social situation, have to deal with this problem all the time and, at an abstract level, they all do it in the same way. On the other hand, at a manifest level, they manipulate the paradoxes that are involved with very diverse kinds of symbolic apparatus.

At rock bottom that is what my kind of social anthropology is all about; it is essentially a demonstration that when an individual progresses through time from social state 'A' to another social state 'B', the progression is always of the continuous/discontinuous kind represented by the sequence '−1', '0', '+1'.

That certainly is what the fashionable style of anthropology known as 'structuralism' is all about.[1] But this book is only concerned with that particular, somewhat technical, issue at one remove. It is not a book about 'structuralism' as such, or even about the many deviations from Lévi-Straussian orthodoxy which are now current; it is a book about the different kinds of anthropological influence which have converged together in my own thinking and led to the particular style of anthropological argument which I now habitually adopt.

I am not addressing myself to anthropologists who already have an established theoretical position and who are prepared to defend their private prejudices to the last ditch.

Rather my imaginary reader is someone like myself at the age of twenty-five to whom learning about anthropology came as an unexpected intrusion into a deceptively well-organized existence.

I myself had a lot of fun learning about anthropology in this non-academic way, doing it first and trying to understand it afterwards, so perhaps there are others who will also get inspiration from this unsystematic approach. Finally a word of apology to half my potential readership. Humankind is male/female, betwixt and between. Anthropologists and book readers are likewise. However, the English language fairly consistently treats 'unmarked' nouns as male rather than female. Ordinarily this does not matter but a male anthropologist, writing in 1980, risks his neck with feminist colleagues if he implies, even by oversight, that either the anthropological observer or the individual who is observed is more likely to be male than female. But I must risk it. A text which is excessively littered with 'he(she)', 'him(her)' expressions becomes unreadable. And anyway why not 'she(he)'? In this book I fairly consistently stick to male pronouns for unmarked category nouns. I should not on that account be rated as a male chauvinist pig.

I suppose that I may fairly claim that some of the ideas that underlie the argument of this book originated with myself but the great majority derive from other people. In a few particular cases I have made this clear in the text but for the most part I have made no attempt to associate a particular argument with its original author.

I have to thank Christine Hugh-Jones and the Syndics of the Cambridge University Press for permission to reprint the passage which appears at pages 146–7. Much of Chapter 2 has appeared in French in my book *Unité de l'homme et autres essais* (Gallimard: 1980), and has been developed from a contribution made to a seminar organized by Professor

Morton Fried at Columbia University in the spring of 1976. The title of Chapter 3 and some bits of the text derive from my 1972 Conway Lecture of which a printed version exists. The figures in Chapters 6 and 7 come from my book *Political Systems of Highland Burma* (1954).

1   The Diversity of Anthropology

If the meaning of words were to be found in their etymology then *anthropology* should be 'the study of man', a monstrous universal form of enquiry which all the books in the world could not suffice to cover, so it is not surprising that most laymen find it difficult to understand just what it is that anthropologists do or why. To make matters worse the professional product now arrives pre-packed under a variety of own-brand labels carrying such titles as physical anthropology, cultural anthropology, social anthropology, cognitive anthropology, symbolic anthropology, medical anthropology, development anthropology, urban anthropology, Marxist anthropology, structuralist anthropology, or what you will. As with other kinds of merchandise the goods inside the package are not so varied as the salesmen would have you believe, but it is all very confusing. What is the common theme behind all these labels?

Some of the labels are more important than others. Two particular polarities deserve special attention from readers of this book. First there is the contrast between the social anthropologists and the cultural anthropologists. The former trace their intellectual descent from Durkheim and Max Weber, the latter from Tylor and the traveller's-tale ethnologists of earlier centuries. Secondly there is the contrast between the empiricists and the rational idealists, between those who aspire to making anthropology a natural science akin to zoology, and who therefore hold that anthropologists should confine their attention to the kinds of fact which can be recorded on videotape or reduced to columns of statistics, and those who argue as if anthropology were a kind of linguistic philosophy in which the ultimate objective is to discover the unconscious structures of the human mind. This latter distinction cuts across most of the brand-name labels I have listed above. It is also relatively recent. It is the direct consequence of a partial assimilation of ideas borrowed from Lévi-Strauss into some of the sub-varieties of both social and cultural anthropology.

My own anthropological practice, which will be reflected throughout this book, rates as social anthropology rather than cultural anthropology. It is empiricist in its derivation from the work of Malinowski and Firth and idealist in its derivation from Lévi-Strauss. My main purpose in the present chapter is to clarify those distinctions though I shall also need to say something about certain other brands of anthropology for which I have much less respect.

Viewed introspectively the concept of 'a study of man' does not seem unduly complicated. Since I can recognize without effort my membership of a particular animal species which the zoologists now call *Homo sapiens*, it is surely only reasonable that I should want to know what is universally true about the members of that species and just how they differ from the members of all other species. It also seems reasonable that, having thus established all the factors which distinguish 'men' from 'non-men', I should go on to make a further inventory of all the possible ways in which men differ, or might differ, among themselves, both in their individual characteristics and as members of groups. I would then end up with a taxonomy of types of men, types of social group, types of civilization, or whatever.

The work of respected professional anthropologists has often taken this form and many introductory textbooks on the subject are still written as if human cultures and/or human societies could be distinguished from each other much as if they were botanical species. This is a fallacy. The diversities of human kind are like the colours of the rainbow; appearances are deceptive; when you look closely at the spectrum the discontinuities disappear. But the issue is important and it needs to be viewed in historical perspective.

The gentlemen scholars of Western Europe and the United States who turned out to be the founding fathers of modern anthropology began to see themselves as a distinct academic species sometime around 1840. Even at that date their interests were very diverse. We can distinguish four main types: anthropologists, ethnologists, archaeologists and philologists.

The anthropologists were avowed heretics. They mostly rejected the unity of mankind postulated in the Bible in favour of a theory that there are a variety of man-like species of which only the white-skinned European is a fully rational human being.

The ethnologists likewise believed that the diverse breeds (races) of man which can be distinguished on the basis of physical appearance are of very different innate capacity, but they fitted their scheme into a biblical framework. They devoted their main attention to the diversity of human customs and their geographical distribution.

The archaeologists were mostly treasure-hunting romantics whose interpretations of their excavations were heavily coloured by their reading of biblical and classical literature but they had already grasped the essential point that when human remains and artifacts are discovered in geological strata laid down prior to the present age this provides us with hard evidence about facts of unrecorded history.

Finally the philologists were very hesitantly coming to accept the possibility that perhaps the Indo-Aryan origins of

Latin and Greek were not the only matters of ultimate interest in the vast uncharted sea of comparative linguistics.

Taken all together this band of amateurs who formed themselves into the first Societies of Anthropology and Ethnology were a quarrelsome crew and, as individuals, they were clearly heading in several different directions; but, in one respect at least, they shared common ground. They were all concerned, as no one had been before, with 'the others', with non-Christians, with man outside the literary heritage of Greece and Rome, and hence with man in the wild, natural man, primitive man, the benighted savage. In practice this bias has remained the delimiting hallmark of academic anthropology. Anthropology has turned out to be not the study of man but the study of primitive man.

Part of the original appeal of this new arrogant and ethnocentric science was that it fitted perfectly with the ethos of the era of European colonial expansion and the westward movement of the American Frontier, for it rested on the basic premise that all non-Europeans are stupid, childish, barbarous and servile by their very nature. Even today the technical jargon of anthropology is heavy with value-loaded implications which stem from its origins in the context of the colonialist world.

As the subject developed, and particularly after it began to receive institutional recognition in museums and universities, the specialists hived off in different directions. Yet for a long while the physical anthropologists, the ethnologists, the archaeologists and the linguists retained a tenuous link under the common banner of 'prehistory'. They all supposed that they were engaged in the reconstruction of the history of periods and peoples for which no written records survive.

The contemporary primitive peoples, who provided most

of the data from which these various brands of anthropologist constructed their theories, were not regarded as interesting in themselves but only because of what they might, by inference, tell us about the distant past. They were 'living fossils'; their savage customs were horrid survivals from antiquity which served to illustrate both the stupidity and the depravity of the beast-like behaviour of our primeval ancestors.

Furthermore, on the assumption that these surviving primitive peoples are primitive in differing degree, it became possible to treat the supposed historical residues as markers of the different rungs of a supposedly universal ladder of human progress at the summit of which was to be found the capitalist society of European Christianity.

The essential absurdity of such ideas was widely recognized at least eighty years ago but because Marx and Engels had taken over an undiluted version of this theory from L. H. Morgan,[1] Marxist anthropologists, both in the Soviet Union and elsewhere, continued, until very recently, to write as if it were firmly established that a universally identical sequence of socio-economic stages has marked the evolution of man's adaptation to his environment and that these stages can be illustrated from still observable ethnographic examples.

And even among anthropologists who now repudiate these nineteenth-century dogmas there is still a marked tendency to write as if there were a clear-cut discontinuity between 'traditional', 'mythopoeic', 'preliterate', 'static' societies (which are studied by anthropologists) and 'modern', 'historical', 'literate', 'progressive' societies (which are studied by historians, sociologists and political scientists).

This is a view which is coming to seem increasingly old-fashioned and which I myself completely reject. It is one of the points of disagreement which distinguishes my style of doing anthropology from that of Lévi-Strauss.

The differences between the primitive societies which anthropologists like to discuss and the modern industrial societies in which most readers of this book are likely to have grown up belong to the level of macro-economics and macro-sociology. At the level of domestic and inter-personal relations with which most people are concerned for most of each working day, the superficial contrasts are simply different transformations of a single complex of ideas about the proper relationship between men and things and men and other men. It is wholly misleading to suppose that people who seem different from 'us' at this level must on that account be archaic in their mental or social organization.

Nevertheless this problem of how far we are all the same and how far we are different is a constant puzzle in all kinds of anthropological enquiry. As I now write the earliest direct evidence for the existence of creatures who were hominids with an upright stance like our own is about 4 million years old. It consists of footprints in congealed volcanic dust. Three individuals were walking together. The two larger, one heavier than the other, walked in a straight line, one behind the other. The other smaller creature ran around in a zig-zag from side to side. Is the imagination running riot if we now say that here was a 'man' and his 'wife' and their 'child'?

The kind of answers we might give to such a question depends on definitions. What constitutes a member of the species *Homo* from a zoological point of view? The experts disagree. The notion of 'wife' is meaningless except in the social context of a community of speaking human beings. So is it possible that these creatures might be described as human beings possessing language and living in some kind of organized society? We cannot possibly know. Yet this visual suggestion of a nuclear family of father, mother and child existing four million years ago is startling and very far removed from the fantasies of sexual promiscuity and 'group marriage' which dominated the thinking of the anthropologists of the Morgan-Engels period.

Throughout prehistory members of our species exhibited a quite remarkable capacity for getting around the map. It would now appear that despite the obstacles of geography there were men of our modern sort in both Australia and the Americas as early as 40,000 years ago. In mainland Africa-Europe-Asia there have been creatures more or less like us for several million years at least. But how like us? We don't know.

The culture and social organization of these long-ago peoples doubtless represented, in a Marxist sense, a socio-economic adaptation to the environment in which they lived. But since that environment was already extremely varied (it included both tropical and arctic climates, forests as well as savannahs, and so on), we must assume that primeval human society was also extremely varied. Of course it would be quite fascinating if we could know what any part of this was like, but we do not know and it is a waste of time to guess. Illustrations from the records of ethnography are wholly irrelevant. The hunter-gatherer societies of remote antiquity need not have resembled in the very least any of those which are now known to us from direct observation.

Some quite recent 'primitive' societies appear to have been notably well adapted to the environments in which they existed at the time when they were first encountered by Europeans but that also is beside the point. The Eskimo and the peoples of Patagonia adapted to very similar sub-arctic environments in entirely different ways. For example, the Eskimo developed very elaborate clothing of great technical sophistication; the Patagonians wore no clothes at all except a loose shoulder cape. Likewise people who live in tropical rain forests do not all have the same kind of society nor have they all adopted the same solutions to the basic technological problems of survival.

Modern ethnography can be used to demonstrate the extreme flexibility of human ingenuity; it cannot tell us anything at all about prehistory. So do not believe what is implied about these matters in the pages of the *American Anthropologist* and *Current Anthropology*.

Another general characteristic of late nineteenth-century anthropology was that the different kinds of specialist all took it for granted that their units of discourse were interchangeable. In particular, the word 'race', as applied to the living population of a particular geographical area, presupposed that the population in question was distinct from all others (a) in its physical characteristics as a sub-species (breed) of the species *Homo*, (b) in its language, (c) in its 'culture' (i.e. customs and material artifacts), and (d) in its historical antecedents.

The scholars of the period wrote as if there were an indefinitely large number of such races of mankind. The common task of all anthropologists was the decipherment of their history. This history once known would allow each race to be placed in its proper position in the general hierarchy of technical, mental and social inferiority.

It was further assumed that, taken as a whole, the intellectual evolution of the human species had been analogous to the maturation of an individual human child. The inferiority of *the others* was essentially a matter of mental incapacity; their ignorant stupidity was that of small children. The paternalistic discipline exercised by their colonial rulers and by their Christian missionary school-masters was thus a form of benevolence.

This general complex of ideas retained its academic respectability until well on into the twentieth century but from about 1900 onwards, both in Europe and in America, more emphasis was given to the study of racial distribution and less to the hierarchy of racial inferiority. Prehistory now developed into a discussion of the past movements of 'peoples' which (so it was said) could be reconstructed from an adroit combination of the study of skull shapes, comparative linguistics, and the distribution of exotic customs such as the mummification of the dead.

I do not exaggerate. In 1926 A. C. Haddon, the distinguished Cambridge anthropologist, wrote to his protégé, A. B. Deacon, while the latter was in the field in Melanesia, urging him to concentrate his ethnological enquiries within the area of religion, secret societies and kinship. At the same time he was expected to collect artifacts for the Cambridge museum, carry out research into the local language, and spend half of each working day gathering elaborate statistics about the shape of people's skulls.[2]

But by this date the failure of the anthropologist's historical endeavour was already widely recognized. In Britain most of the younger anthropologists were adapting their thinking to a new fashion which affirmed that the goal of anthropology was not historical reconstruction at all but the establishment of a general theory of comparative sociology.

This new style, sociological anthropology, was mainly derived from the work which had developed in Paris from 1893 onwards under the auspices of Emile Durkheim, but, at one remove, it also reflected the dialogue between Max Weber and the Marxists about the role of 'rationality' in modern bureaucratic industrial societies and about the relationship, causal or otherwise, between changes in religious ideology (e.g. the emergence of 'the protestant ethic' in the sixteenth century) and changes in economic structure (e.g. the development of wage labour capitalism).

In this new fashion the supposedly characteristic indi-
cators of primitive societies, e.g. strange kinship practices,
magic, witchcraft, exotic customs of all kinds, were no longer
seen as illustrations of the innate childish stupidity of
savages but as reflections of a special mode of 'primitive
mentality' which was, in some obscure way, functionally
interdependent with the economic non-rationality of 'traditional' societies.

This was not a clear-cut debate. It developed over many
years and in some respects still continues.

For the earlier anthropologists the contrast between
'primitive' and 'civilized' rested on a presumed difference in
the mental type of the individual; for the sociological
thinkers the difference lay in the type of society into which
the individual happened to be born.

The former convention found its final popular expression
in the pages of Frazer's *The Golden Bough* where belief in
magic and the divinity of kings is held to demonstrate a lack
of capacity for rational thinking that has now become
almost second nature for adult, educated, modern
Europeans. Though, to be fair, Frazer was quite willing to
admit that educated modern Europeans are not always as
rational as they themselves would like to believe. But, for the
sociologists, it was not a question of whether the individual
was irrational or rational, childish or adult, uneducated or
educated, but rather of *how* the individual had been educated
('socialized'). Hence the anthropologist should concentrate
his attention upon the variety of social matrices within which
individuals grow up.

Quite early in the century Lévy-Bruhl in France and Pareto
in Italy, starting from independent positions, had both come
to recognize that the opposition between logical-rational-
experimentally valid, on the one hand, and illogical-
irrational-scientifically false, on the other, represents a crude

oversimplification of the possible alternatives. In an appreciative comment on these insights, published in 1936, Evans-Pritchard wrote:

> Lévy-Bruhl saw that primitive thought is coherent and that savages make valid inferences from propositions even though their propositions are not in accord with experience but are dictated by culture and contained in beliefs which are demonstrably false from a logico-experimental standpoint.[3]

The intellectual relativism which is implicit in that assessment continues to be hotly debated and lies at the root of many of the current disagreements between the 'rationalists' and the 'empiricists' among contemporary social anthropologists.

The continuing, if indirect, influence of Lévy-Bruhl's ideas is also shown by the respect which is accorded to Lévi-Strauss' theorizing about 'mytho-logics' and 'thought in the wild' (*la pensée sauvage*),[4] as well as by the frequency with which contemporary British anthropologists are liable to refer to the 'language game' and 'family resemblance' arguments in Wittgenstein's *Philosophical Investigations*.

Unlike their nineteenth-century predecessors nearly all contemporary professional anthropologists have had direct experience of fieldwork. Thus they know at first hand that when arguments are conducted in an alien language in an alien social context the opposition entailed in our English 'true/false' may become far more complicated than the logic of Aristotle would suggest. But in 1914 such ideas would have seemed very strange and their partial adoption by the younger generation of anthropologists amounted to an intellectual revolution.

It was a revolution which shattered the already fragile

unity of anthropology. The social anthropologists moved away from the rest. Their rejection of conjectural history separated them from the archaeologists. In laying stress on social environment as against innate predisposition they eliminated the word 'race' from their vocabulary and thus inhibited communication with the physical anthropologists and the zoologists. But within the sociological camp itself a further bifurcation developed between those who took their affiliation with sociology seriously and called themselves social anthropologists, and those who retained a hankering for reconstructed history and eventually came to describe themselves as cultural anthropologists.

This last distinction which seems trivial to some and fundamental to others has now become tangled up with the allocation of jobs in university departments. Moreover, because the history of the matter has been different in Britain, France and the United States, a clarification of the terminology presents considerable difficulties. However, since I feel rather strongly that I am a social anthropologist and not a cultural anthropologist, I must make the attempt.

Social anthropology

The term social anthropology was a British invention. It was very seldom used prior to the First World War. Sir James Frazer was appointed to an honorific Chair of Social Anthropology at the University of Liverpool as early as 1907 but, in retrospect, this seems anomalous. Frazer's anthropology now seems very unlike the social anthropology of later British writers all of whom took their sociological bearings from Durkheim, either direct, or at second hand through Malinowski or Radcliffe-Brown, or both.

In the period 1907–22 the dominant intellectual influence

in British academic anthropology did not come from Frazer but from Haddon's close friend W. H. R. Rivers, the brilliant Cambridge polymath whose activities and interests ranged from experimental psychology to anthropological fieldwork and from global conjectural history to the intricacies of Melanesian kinship terminologies.

Although Rivers was responsible for a number of very important innovations in the technique of field research and although the emphasis of much of his own fieldwork was sociological, his main anthropological concerns during the later phases of his career were essentially those of the old-style ethnologists. He became preoccupied with the grand-scale reconstruction of unrecorded history. The paradoxical consequence was that, after he died unexpectedly in 1922, his lasting influence on British anthropology was largely by inversion. The next generation avoided writing about either speculative history or the analysis of kinship terminologies for no better reason than that Rivers' exercises in these areas had come to seem entirely bizarre!

At this period the Rivers' style anthropology that was thus repudiated was always referred to as 'ethnology' and contrasted with the more modern style which was called 'social anthropology'. By contrast, in the United States, the only people who ever claimed to be social anthropologists were former pupils of Radcliffe-Brown who had come under his influence either during the period when he held a Professorial Chair at Sydney (1926–31) or later when he was at Chicago (1931–9).

For British anthropology, 1922 proved to be a watershed. It was the year of Rivers' death. It was also the year of publication both of Radcliffe-Brown's *The Andaman Islanders*, with its very Durkheimian treatment of ritual value, and of Malinowski's *Argonauts of the Western Pacific*, the brilliant study of the Trobriand system of inter-island exchange known as the Kula, which was to leave an indelible mark on the future practice of all styles of sociological anthropology.

Rivers' death proved to be Malinowski's opportunity. From the time that he began to teach at the London School of Economics in 1924 until his departure for America in 1938 he completely dominated the British anthropological scene. In the process he earned a great deal of hostility both from his own most able pupils and from colleagues in a variety of fields. In anthropology, his immediate influence was to shift the bias of interest away from conjectural history to the techniques of field research.

The intermittent visits which Malinowski had paid to the island of Kiriwina between 1914 and 1918 added up to about two years in all. Much of this time was spent in the village community of Omarakana where Malinowski became intimately acquainted with many of the individual inhabitants. This simple, unplanned circumstance later led to a fundamental change in research method.

Most earlier field anthropologists, including Rivers and Boas, had worked through interpreters and had obtained the bulk of their ethnographic information either by working with transcribed texts or through relatively short formal interviews with specially selected 'good informants' who were paid for their services. By contrast, Malinowski became highly fluent in the vernacular and had himself been a participant observer of most of the Trobriand activities which he described.

The gain in quality which resulted from this combination of direct observation, use of the vernacular, and personal participation was very obvious and versions of Malinowski's innovative procedures have subsequently become part of the general practice of anthropological field research in all parts of the world.

When modern anthropologists outside the Soviet Union refer to 'fieldwork' they mean essentially what Malinowski meant except that advances in technology, e.g. Polaroid cameras, tape-recorders, videotape etc., have greatly enlarged the possibilities that are open to the research worker.

These developments, especially the close attention paid to the synchronic functional interdependence of institutions operating within a single social context, led to corresponding changes in the style in which anthropologists presented their findings.

Whereas their British predecessors (e.g. Tylor, Frazer, Hartland) had regularly compared customs quite independently of their context and were thus quite happy to mention within a single paragraph half a dozen tribal peoples ranging from China to Peru and spread over several millennia of history, the writings of Malinowski and his pupils nearly always took the form of detailed monographs relating to a single society narrowly defined in topic, time and space.

For example, Raymond Firth's classic studies of the Tikopia, which include major monographs on the themes of kinship, economics, religion and mythology as well as dozens of shorter articles relating to every aspect of Tikopia social life, are concerned with the activities as a population of less than 1300 individuals who, in 1929, occupied a small Pacific island of about three square miles in area. The recurrent theme throughout this massive corpus of published materials is the demonstration of how the ethnographic details all dovetail together. Firth is meticulous in recording the fine details of the case but his theoretical interest is to show how it all fits together into a single functioning whole.

Eventually this fashion also became dominant in the United States even among writers who formally rejected most of the tenets of Malinowski's functionalism. But in France the comparative structuralism of Lévi-Strauss still calls for a piecemeal attitude towards ethnography which has much more in common with the style of Frazer than that of Malinowski. This however is much less true of most of Lévi-Strauss' successors.

During the period 1926–45 the labels 'social anthropology' and 'functionalist anthropology' were virtually synonymous. Both terms carried negative as well as positive implications. Functionalist anthropologists concerned themselves with the interdependence of institutions within a limited context of time and space; conversely they did *not* concern themselves with the speculative reconstruction of historical process.

But the functionalist anthropologists were not all of one breed. Although outsiders tended to apply the label quite indiscriminately to the disciples of both Malinowski and Radcliffe-Brown and although some of the earlier writings of these two gurus had much in common, they and their followers later became sharply opposed. This is not surprising for they had entirely different personalities and, from the start, each had adopted his own definition of what the term 'function' was supposed to mean.

For Malinowski the central issue of anthropology was the problem which faces every fieldworker: How should one interpret the bizarre quality which pervades so much of the behaviour which is encountered in the exotic settings which anthropologists usually choose as the arena for their research? The essence of his answer was that as soon as the social context is fully understood the bizarre quality disappears. In context, the various aspects of human social behaviour – domestic, economic, legal, political, magico-religious, technological – fit together and 'make sense'.

'Making sense' for Malinowski here meant 'common

sense', practical utility as the anthropological observer perceives it, even if this might sometimes mean giving a very peculiar twist to the notion of utility.

Up to a point this line of argument is acceptable and important even if it can sometimes seem naïve. It is always highly desirable that the fieldworker should rid himself of the notion that there is something altogether extraordinary about the situation he is observing.

'Magic' is not a strange mystery which can only be encountered in traveller's tales and medieval romances. Everyone who shows above average competence at producing a cup of coffee or growing tomatoes achieves his results by 'magic' (or as we usually say 'art') rather than by strict adherence to scientific principle. In other words it is crucial for the fieldworker to recognize that what the observer finds strange and mysterious the actor may regard as entirely obvious.

But for Malinowski this was not enough. He felt he needed a causal explanation for the behaviours he observed and he believed that such an explanation was provided by the dogma that every social institution must, in one way or another, serve the immediate practical needs of the human individual.

On this issue Malinowski was quite un-Durkheimian. He was still assuming that the object of anthropological enquiry was to understand the nature of man rather than the nature of human society. He believed that if the research worker can come to understand the fitting together of institutions in a really comprehensive way, even in just one social context, he will have learnt something of fundamental importance about human nature everywhere. Malinowski viewed the integration of society from the inside rather than the outside; as the consequence of individual self-interest rather than of social necessity.

This approach to the observable facts can often prove very illuminating but the trouble is that, in Malinowski's presentation, the argument is banal. It is self-evidently true but trivial. In the last analysis the basic needs of the individual are biological; the need to survive and to procreate. But the functionalist dogma then becomes a kind of just-so story. For after all if social institutions did not make it possible for individuals to survive and procreate there would be no social institutions anyway!

In the outcome Malinowski's explanations for the oddities of ethnographic data were often very similar to those which are currently being advanced by the sociobiologist followers of E. O. Wilson. Wilson's dogma is that all custom is the outcome of a process of Darwinian adaptation to the environment which serves, in some sense or other, to maximize the chance that an individual's genetic endowment will be perpetuated in the gene pool of the collective society.[5] It should not be difficult to see that this is again a just-so story borrowed from Dr Pangloss. Everything is for the best in the best of all possible worlds. But as a form of 'explanation' this kind of thing rates rather low.

Radcliffe-Brown's functionalism was very different. His performances as a fieldworker in the Andaman Islands, Africa and Australia had been notably undistinguished and, unlike Malinowski, he does not seem to have had much interest in the complex problems of translation and interpretation that fieldwork necessarily entails. His famous account of the Andamanese value system is an exercise in Durkheimian exegesis rather than a felt experience. He was essentially a stay-at-home theorist. He claimed that social anthropology was 'a generalizing science', 'a comparative sociology' which was expected to arrive at universally valid 'laws' concerning human society by means of the systematic comparison of the structure of total social systems.

Although Radcliffe-Brown had begun his study of anthropology at Cambridge, where in 1904 he was a pupil of Rivers, his subsequent academic career until 1937 was peripatetic and always outside Britain. He thus had little face-to-face interaction with Malinowski. His functionalism was in the tradition established by Durkheim's *De La Division du Travail Social* (1893) and most of his ideas can be seen to derive from a wide, if somewhat insensitive, reading of contributions to Durkheim's journal *Année Sociologique*. Following in this convention Radcliffe-Brown wrote of society as a thing in itself, a self-sustaining organism or system which already exists when the individual is born into it and which constrains the freedom of the individual through a complex structure of jural rules and sanctions which are implicit (rather than explicit) in the traditional mythology and ceremonial of the people concerned. He saw Malinowski's 'common sense' functionalist explanations as an example of the 'danger that the ethnologist may interpret the beliefs of a native people not by reference to *their* mental life but by reference to his own'. This may be fair criticism but it could equally well be levelled against Radcliffe-Brown's own comments on the beliefs of the Andamanese!

Like Malinowski, Radcliffe-Brown was concerned with the nature of social integration. Why do human beings co-operate together within a social matrix? Malinowski looked at the problem from the inside and came up with a dogma of individual self-interest; Radcliffe-Brown looked at it from the outside and laid emphasis on what he saw as a diversity of types of integration each of which finds expression in a distinctive, yet coherent, system of belief and ceremonial practice.

As a derivation from this model Radcliffe-Brown held that the first task of a scientific and sociological anthropology should be to establish a taxonomy of types of society classified according to their internal structural organization. The imagery was zoological and anatomical. Societies with segmentary unilineal descent groups were to be distinguished as species from societies stratified by social class much as mammals are distinguished from fish.

In this version of the social anthropological style, which subsequently came to be described as 'structural-functionalism' (in order to distinguish it from the plain functionalism of the Malinowskians), the central issue was that of social continuity. The anthropologist's task was not to discover how customs serve the (biological) needs of the individual but to understand how social structures persist through time.

Social structure was here taken to mean the articulation of a set of clearly definable and directly observable social institutions which were considered to constitute the basic framework of the society concerned. The *function* of such an institution was formally defined as the part that it played in the maintenance of the system as a whole, on the analogy that, in a mammalian body, the function of the heart is to pump blood through the circulating network of arteries and veins.

To a limited extent the structural-functionalists based their generalizations on cross-cultural comparison but, unlike the Frazerians, their comparisons were of total systems rather than of the elements of such systems. They were just as insistent as their Malinowskian rivals that no valid historical inferences can be derived from the study of isolated 'traits' such as peculiarities of kinship terminology, rules or marriage, burial customs, principles of descent, patterns of residence, and so on.

In Britain studies of this latter sort had been characteristic of the now despised 'ethnology' of the Haddon-Rivers era, but work of an essentially similar kind continued to have its devotees in the United States for many years and quite recently it has reappeared in the work of British social anthropologists of high repute. Latter-day examples are provided by Murdock in *Social Structure* (1949) and Goody in *Production and Reproduction* (1976). Though I am not an advocate of sectarianism in anthropology I do not myself consider that this particular blend of sociological and ethnological methods can produce any worthwhile results.

But in any case, at the period I am now discussing, which was the period at which I myself first became acquainted with British anthropologists, the trend was just the other way; the gulf between the 'social anthropologists' and the 'ethnologists' was widening all the time.

In Britain, in the late 1940s, it was widely believed that the pursuit of conjectural history in an 'ethnological' style was the type characteristic of all American academic anthropology. In 1946 the various British functionalists briefly suspended their local internecine feuds to form themselves into The Association of Social Anthropologists of the British Commonwealth. This grandiose and chauvinistic title was intended to assert very emphatically that they did *not* wish to be thought of as 'ethnologists' or 'cultural anthropologists' in the American sense. However, subsequent developments on both sides of the Atlantic and in other parts of the world have made the distinction seem much less clear-cut.

A key factor here was the fact that when Lévi-Strauss came to develop his spectacularly successful revitalization of French anthropology he used quite a different set of terminological conventions. In a paper originally published in 1949, which now forms the first chapter of *Structural Anthropology* (1963), he told his French readers that 'ethnology' (*ethnologie*) embraces both 'social anthropology' and 'cultural anthropology' which are barely distinguishable. Social anthropology is 'the study of institutions considered as systems of representations' (i.e. beliefs, sentiments and norms common to members of society), while cultural anthropology is 'the study of techniques which implement social life (and sometimes also the study of institutions considered as such techniques)'.

Lévi-Strauss avoided placing himself in either of these somewhat opaque categories though his frequent claim that his own brand of anthropology is derivative of that of Boas and Lowie would suggest he considers himself a cultural anthropologist. On the other hand, on the basis of his own definitions, his practice with regard to the study of kinship and his later writings about *La Pensée sauvage* and *Mythologiques* seem to put him, in some respects at least, among the social anthropologists.

The converse to this ambiguity also applies. During the past twenty years British social anthropologists and American cultural anthropologists alike have often been greatly influenced by Lévi-Strauss' 'structuralism' but without noticeably reducing the width of the Atlantic ocean!

Lévi-Strauss' 1949 paper also crossed the wires in another sense for it contrasted history and anthropology in a quite different way from that in which the social anthropologists had rejected diachronic conjectural history in favour of synchronic sociology.

According to Lévi-Strauss, anthropology is concerned with the 'unconscious nature of natural phenomena' whereas the historian keeps 'his eyes fixed on concrete and specific activities'. Anthropology and history are complementary fields but quite distinct: 'The anthropologist is, above all, interested in unwritten data, not so much because the peoples he studies are incapable of writing, but because that with which he is principally concerned differs from everything men ordinarily think of recording on stone or paper.'

This is an important statement. I would suppose that the majority of professional anthropologists throughout the world must share my own view that the suggestion that anthropology is solely or even primarily concerned with unconscious mentalist phenomena is totally unacceptable. But on this issue Lévi-Strauss has made many converts both among the social anthropologists and among the cultural anthropologists (where they often distinguish themselves as 'symbolic anthropologists').

Finally, from the British point of view (as at 1949), Lévi-Strauss made the confusion worse by using the concept of structure in a transformational sense which is familiar to philosophers and mathematicians but far removed from the notion of empirical articulation employed by Radcliffe-Brown. This had the consequence that, at that period, most British social anthropologists entirely misunderstood the nature of the Lévi-Straussian endeavour.

I shall have more to say about Lévi-Strauss' structuralist arguments later on but for the moment I am concerned with the original orthodoxies of the social anthropologists.

Along with their emphasis on the functional interdependence of institutions they took over from Durkheim the curious idea that there is something intrinsically virtuous about functional integration. A society in which, overall, the various institutions are *not* in homeostatic, stable equilibrium was considered to be in a pathological condition and threatened with imminent collapse.

One of the major weaknesses of the Durkheimian model of society is rather obvious. Societies were treated as naturally existing, self-sustaining systems with closed boundaries. But in real life our use of the word society is such that an individual can readily move out of one society and into another. Furthermore, depending upon how you specify criteria of membership, a single individual may be regarded as a member of several different societies at the same time.

The early social anthropologists recognized the problem but somehow managed to persuade themselves that it was unimportant. One consequence of this was that social anthropological theory in the 1940s was markedly conservative. It was presupposed from the start that all observable facts within the social field under investigation must fit together like the gear wheels of a watch. There can be no loose ends; radical change always implies breakdown. It was axiomatic that, taken as a whole, any temporary disruption to the pattern of organization will be self-correcting. The model thus excluded the possibility of evolutionary development and the anthropologists concerned were logically compelled to imagine that the social systems they observed had been like that since time immemorial.

The monographs by Firth on Tikopia (a small island in Western Polynesia) and by Fortes on the Tallensi (a people of Northern Ghana) are among the major classics of social anthropology. The original books were based on fieldwork carried out in 1929 and 1934–7 respectively. Both these former pupils of Malinowski and associates of Radcliffe-Brown have visited the locations of their original research on several subsequent occasions. Firth has even published a book entitled *Social Change in Tikopia* based on a re-study made in 1952–3. It is clear that, in the interval between their first and later visits, the economic basis of society and the general level of technological gadgetry available in ordinary life had changed very dramatically, yet both authors have given the impression that, despite appearances, the fundamentals of Tikopia and Tallensi society had remained just as they were before. But this is not surprising since, for an orthodox functionalist, the study of social continuity is what it is all about!

Most social anthropologists, including myself, should still be rated as 'functionalists' though not in this primeval, pre-1940, sense, but before I attempt an account of later developments I must go back a bit and say something, if only rather briefly, about the kind of anthropologist that I am not.

Cultural anthropology

At the present time most American-style textbooks of anthropology adopt some version of Lévi-Strauss' 1949 synthesis and imply that the distinction between social anthropology (mostly British) and cultural anthropology (mostly American) is just a matter of changing the label on the can. There is more to it than that.

If, as an anthropologist, you are planning a period of field research, it doesn't perhaps matter very much whether you have been trained as a social anthropologist or as a cultural anthropologist. In either case you will need the same sort of equipment and when you finally get into the field you will try to do much the same sort of thing. And in either case you will still be faced with essentially the same problems of interpretation and translation as those which worried Malinowski sixty years ago.

But in the final outcome the fieldwork monographs of social anthropologists and cultural anthropologists usually look very different. The two kinds of specialist come from different intellectual traditions and they look at their materials in quite different ways. The crux of this difference is that where the social anthropologists are still carrying on a dialogue with Durkheim and Max Weber the cultural anthropologists are still arguing with Tylor. To understand what is involved we need to go back to the beginning.

The anthropologist's first concern is to distinguish the characteristics of man from non-man. Until the middle of the nineteenth century it was a dangerous heresy to challenge the theological dogma that the distinction is clear-cut: man, being fashioned in the image of God, is other than a mere animal. But right from the start the anthropologists needed a concept which would express this otherness. *Culture* as opposed to *nature* was made to serve this purpose.

The origin of the distinction goes a long way back and need not concern us, but the analogy is plain. When a man cultivates his fields he creates a man-made world out of a 'natural' substratum; 'nature' here being taken to mean that which would exist anyway even if there were no men around to alter it.

At a material level this usage creates no great difficulty. We look around us and see a world made up of roads and fields and houses and man-made apparatus of all kinds. These are all products of human culture. But it is the *form* that is cultural; the stuff of which these things are made is natural.

However when we turn to the human actor, as distinct from his artifacts, matters become more complicated. Where do we draw the line between the humanity and the animality of man?

The fashion by which the opposition culture/nature was extended to cover moral values as well as material things was a development of the latter part of the nineteenth century when the values of materialist capitalism went almost unchallenged. At that date (and for a long time afterwards) the basic anthropological definition of man was that he was a toolmaker.

Thus Tylor (1871) followed up his celebrated catch-all definition by which 'Culture or civilization, taken in its wide ethnographic sense, is that complex whole which includes knowledge, belief, art, morals, law, custom, and any other capabilities and habits acquired by man as a member of society' with the assertion that 'the first step in the study of civilization is to dissect it into details and to classify these into their proper groups'. The 'proper groups' turn out to be weapons, textile arts, myths, rites and ceremonies, in that order. A similar list a little later in the book has 'special dress, special tools and weapons, special laws of marriage and property, special moral and religious doctrines'.[6]

The priority here given to man-made material things is all the more striking when one considers that in the previous century, 'the Age of Reason', the scholars of the Enlightenment had mostly taken it for granted that what distinguishes man from brute is that men have language and other animals do not.

Since Tylor's day the anthropologist's concept of culture has undergone many transformations and there is no present-day consensus about how the term should be used but one of the shared characteristics of those who rate themselves as cultural anthropologists (as distinct from social anthropologists) is that they continue to write as if culture were a kind of clothing which is quite separate from the human beings who are clothed. Further, they still seem to accept Tylor's formula that 'the first step in the study of culture is to dissect it into details and to classify these into their proper groups'. By contrast, although social anthropologists may also write about culture, they do not ordinarily treat it as a separable thing in itself made up of separable component parts ('traits').

On the other hand the cultural anthropologists are now divided among themselves over issues which are similar to those which marked the separation of the nineteenth-century social evolutionists (e.g., Tylor, Morgan, Marx-

Engels), who were materialists, from their eighteenth-century predecessors (e.g., Vico, Rousseau) who were rationalist idealists.

Crudely stated, the argument is about whether toolmaking or language is the more fundamental. Is this 'thing in itself', culture, to be 'explained' by considering objective facts about the technical adaptation of man to his environment? Or is culture a product of the human imagination which exists only in the mind rather than as a material interface between man and the world of nature?

This book is about social anthropology rather than cultural anthropology and in any case I am not competent to distinguish between all the different styles of contemporary cultural anthropology – symbolic anthropology, cognitive anthropology, bio-cultural anthropology and so on – but the total range is very wide.

At one extreme the variations include the cultural materialism of Marvin Harris, who holds that all peculiarities of culture can be and should be explained by reference to local variations in man's adaptation to the physical environment, e.g., cannibalism is an adaptive response to protein deficiency![7] At the other, the symbolic anthropology of David Schneider, who defines culture as 'a system of symbols and meanings',[8] is preoccupied with culture as a language-based process of thought and apparently excludes altogether the more practical aspects of its material manifestations such as the utility of the clothes we wear and of the houses we live in.

I am personally a good deal more sympathetic to Schneider's approach than to that of Harris but that is not the point. It is not a question of how far either of these scholars is right or wrong for clearly they are thinking about the problems of anthropology in quite different ways, and, in any case, their problems are not my problems. This book is not an introduction or guide to cultural anthropology of any sort. And that needs to be stressed. Social anthropology and cultural anthropology are not just two alternative names for the same form of academic enquiry.

Units of culture and society

There is, however, one aspect of cultural anthropology about which something more has to be said. Tylor wrote about 'culture' in the singular; present-day anthropologists regularly write about 'societies' and 'cultures' in the plural.

The 'societies' usage is mostly just a manner of speaking. The sensible social anthropologist does not now delude himself into thinking that each of the social units which he describes as 'a society' is comparable to every other. Most of what Radcliffe-Brown wrote on this topic is best forgotten.

In practice, 'a society' means a political unit of some sort which is territorially defined. Very often it is a segment of some larger political unit which might, in some slightly different context, also be described as 'a society'. The boundaries of such units are usually vague. They are determined by operational convenience rather than rational argument. But they are objective.

The members of 'a society' at any one time are a specifiable set of individuals who can be found together in one part of the map and who share common interests of some sort. I am not a purist on these matters. It makes perfectly good sense to talk about Tikopia society, or Tallensi society, or Chinese society so long as, *but only so long as*, we do not imagine that the Tikopia – 1300 people living on an island of three square miles – are, in any meaningful sense, directly comparable to the Chinese – 600 million people occupying half a continent. Unfortunately it is all too easy to find highly respected anthropological publications which make comparisons of just this sort all the time!

But I find the notion of a plurality of cultures much more difficult. I can understand what might be meant by Tikopia culture or Tallensi culture but I fail to see how these manifestations of culture (civilization) in different parts of the map can be distinguished as isolated things which are somehow comparable to one another regardless of the fact that the human populations concerned are wholly incommensurate.

Yet there is a long tradition among cultural anthropologists of all kinds that cultures can be compared and contrasted in just this way. The fashion was started by Tylor in a paper published in 1889 which is often cited as a landmark;[9] the first attempt to use statistical comparison in cultural anthropology and therefore the beginnings of a truly 'scientific' study of culture. And things have gone on that way ever since. But I myself find the whole ideology quite incomprehensible. In the HRAF tabulations the characteristics of Tikopia culture and Chinese culture are itemized trait by trait as if they were segmentable units of just the same kind.

I must admit that I do not understand the language. When Schneider (1968) wrote about American culture – meaning, apparently, the culture of the whole of the United States – he cannot possibly have intended to refer to the same kind of entity as Roberts (1964), who was comparing the cultures of four North American tribes; but just where the difference is supposed to lie I do not know.

The issue is of importance for a social anthropologist because there is a common assumption, which is sometimes quite explicit, that the boundaries of cultural units are the subjective counterpart of the objective boundaries of 'societies'. For example, the materialist Harris, following in the footsteps of Tylor, has claimed that 'culture . . . refers to the learned repertory of thought and actions exhibited by members of social groups',[10] while Geertz, whose position is much closer to Schneider's idealism, makes the categorical, but quite unverifiable, assertion that 'all Balinese share the same general beliefs, the same overall world-view, the same broad ideas of how their society is or should be arranged'.[11] Geertz is here writing about Balinese 'culture' as the counterpart of Balinese 'society'.

This style of argument makes it axiomatic that every 'society' ('social group') is culturally homogeneous. But, from a sociological point of view, this is totally misleading. Almost all empirical societies (i.e. political units which are territorially delimited) are socially stratified – by 'social class', by 'hereditary caste', by 'hierarchy of rank' etc. – and each stratum in the system is marked by its own distinctive cultural attributes – linguistic usages, manners, styles of dress, food, housing, etc. The decoding of such systems of symbolic representation is the primary task of the social anthropologist. But not only is there no uniformity of symbolic usage throughout any one society but the cultural differentia that are thus employed are highly unstable over time, as our concept of 'fashion' clearly shows. Furthermore, as Marxists are never tired of pointing out, class consciousness need not coincide with class membership however defined.

So beware. When you encounter an anthropologist who writes about cultures in the plural, or who writes as if the culture of a society were like a unique set of clothes in which each garment can be separately described independently of any of the others, watch out! In all probability the *découpage*, the discontinuity which separates one culture from another or one cultural 'trait' from another, exists only in the mind of the anthropologist observer.

Credo

So let me get back to social anthropology and, more particularly, to my own particular style of social anthropology.

I myself was first indoctrinated into anthropology by Malinowski and Firth. That is to say I was, at the outset, a 'pure', empirical, functionalist. Much later I was greatly influenced by the very unempirical structuralism of Lévi-Strauss. This came about because Lévi-Strauss' first magnum opus, *The Elementary Structures of Kinship*, the first French edition of which was published in 1949, makes great use of the ethnography of the Kachin of North Burma, a people among whom I had lived during much of the period 1939–45.

I knew from first-hand experience that a great deal of the ethnography on which Lévi-Strauss had relied was quite inaccurate, but I also knew from first-hand experience that a number of his novel insights concerning this society were very penetrating.

My book *Political Systems of Highland Burma*, besides arguing against the then conventional view that the boundaries of society and the boundaries of culture can be treated as coincident, is also organized as a kind of dialogue between the empiricism of Malinowski and the rationalism of Lévi-Strauss and these two contrasted strands of my thinking should be apparent to the reader in all my later writings.

But during a large part of my academic career the Malinowskian functionalism was out of fashion. The dominant clique among British social anthropologists were the structural-functionalist followers of Radcliffe-Brown, Fortes and Gluckman in particular, and, at least for a time, Evans-Pritchard.

I first met Fortes in 1938 shortly after he returned from his first period of field research among the Tallensi and, after 1953, I was his colleague in Cambridge. Although I was fairly consistently unsympathetic to the style of argument adopted by the structural-functionalists it is clear that, even if only in negative reaction, I was greatly influenced by what they said and wrote; so I need now to give a further summary of some of the key points in their position.

The central dogmas of the school are spelled out in the editorial Introduction by Fortes and Evans-Pritchard to *African Political Systems* (1940) and, in less lucid fashion, by Radcliffe-Brown's own Introduction to the companion volume, *African Systems of Kinship and Marriage* (1950).

In line with both Durkheim and Weber the structural-functionalists of this period believed that human societies can all be slotted, without much distortion of the facts, into a very limited number of ideal types. The scheme was dyadic: centralized states were first opposed to acephalous stateless societies; then, among the latter, structures based on the articulation of unilineal descent groups were contrasted with bilateral kinship systems articulated around 'kindreds'; then matrilineal systems were contrasted with patrilineal systems, and so on.

The schema was restricted in its functionalist scope. The authors concerned paid little attention to economics. The typology was developed, almost exclusively, from a consideration of the role of formal and informal rules relating to social identity and marriage in generating a sense of political solidarity. The religious aspects of social life were given some consideration but treated only as expressions of the values underlying the structure of politics and kinship.

As noted earlier, it was assumed as a matter of dogma that the functional integration of social institutions was intrinsically stable, that is to say that, in the absence of external political interference everything will go on as before. This whole framework of ideas is of course directly at variance with the basic postulates of Marxism which insist categorically, not only that political structure is an epiphenomenon of the mode of production but that internal contradictions are inevitable and that these contradictions are the principal generative source of historical development.

It is thus somewhat curious that a number of the most prominent structural-functionalists, including Gluckman and several of his pupils, had decided personal leanings towards Marxism.

Most of the anthropologists concerned were Africanists and they tended to exaggerate the degree to which principles of organization which are widespread in Africa have application in other parts of the world. Thus they paid too much attention to segmentary lineage organizations and too little to the great variety of forms of bilateral (cognatic) kinship. They accepted without challenge the thesis, current among anthropologists ever since the days of Morgan, that, in small-scale pre-industrial societies, kinship always provides the basic fabric of society, in the sense that, in one way or another, every individual in the social system perceives himself (or herself) as kin to every other.

Likewise they took over from Morgan the universality of the distinction between consanguinity and affinity. All those who are my kinsmen, in the most general sense, are either 'consanguines', true kinsmen by blood or common substance, or 'affines', related to me only by marriage. They recognized, as Morgan had largely failed to do, that the opposed categories refer to ideas rather than to biological facts or manifest legal contracts, but, unlike some of the latter-day 'cognitive' and 'symbolic' anthropologists, they paid just as close attention to what they observed to be actually happening as to the patterning of ideas about what ought to be happening.

Collectively these authors demonstrated very convincingly how the lineage principle, the doctrine of presumed consanguinity based on descent through links of one sex only from a common ancestor, can function as the basis for an ideology of political solidarity; but they ignored, or even expressly denied, the alternative non-Marxist possibility that political solidarity in kinship-based society might be based on a doctrine of permanent affinity, i.e. that lineages as wholes might not only be linked in a permanent sibling relationship, as happens in any segmentary lineage system, but also by such relationships as father-in-law/son-in-law or mother-in-law/daughter-in-law.

The kinship theory developed by Lévi-Strauss from 1945 onwards, in which I became especially interested because of its relevance to my Kachin materials, had exactly the opposite characteristics. It was concerned with the patterning of ideas in the mind rather than with facts on the ground and, from an empirical point of view, it paid too much attention to structures of permanent affinity ('alliance'), which represented a very restricted version of what Durkheim had called 'organic solidarity', and too little to the alternative principle of hierarchical segmentation, which Durkheim had called 'mechanical solidarity'.

Incidentally, in contrast to structural-functionalism with its emphatic anti-historicist bias, the kinship theory expounded in Lévi-Strauss (1949) was, in a certain off-beat fashion, a kind of modified Marxism. 'Kinship structure' replaced 'mode of production' as the *basis* of the social system, but the Marxist dogma of the inevitability of internal contradiction serving as a motor force for evolutionary change was retained.

I find it very odd that Lévi-Strauss should have argued in

this fashion for, as we have already seen, he was at this date already beginning to assert that the data of anthropology and the data of history are of quite different kinds. Moreover he has subsequently repeatedly declared that the societies to which his arguments about elementary structures can be applied are 'societies without history'.

On the other hand there have also been occasions when Lévi-Strauss has proclaimed that he is a Marxist, and, in France, some of his closest followers, e.g. Maurice Godelier, have achieved, at least to their own satisfaction, a complete doctrinal synthesis between the materialism of Marx and the rational idealism of Lévi-Strauss.

But the controversy which came to divide the followers of Radcliffe-Brown from the followers of Lévi-Strauss, in which I increasingly found myself being pushed into the Lévi-Straussian camp, went far deeper than the superficial polemics between the functionalists and the historicists or between the lineage theorists and the alliance theorists. The real issue concerned levels of abstraction. It was an argument about empiricism and idealism and the kind of 'reality' that can be attributed to the anthropologist's models of society.

The structural-functionalist programme was to arrive at generalized sociological laws by comparing total social systems. This is a highly reductionist procedure yet the anthropologists concerned thought of themselves as strict empiricists. They claimed that the representations of particular societies which they contrasted as species types were direct derivations from first-hand observations in the field; they were not just models in the mind to which convenient ethnographic evidence had been made to fit. Thus, in the orthodox view, the 'paradigms' by which Evans-Pritchard and Fortes illustrated the segmentary lineage structures of the Nuer and the Tallensi were entirely different in kind from the permutation models by which Lévi-Strauss later exemplified his abstract concepts of 'generalized' and 'restricted' exchange.

In the eyes of my British colleagues my own heresy lay precisely there. In writing about the Kachin I treated the principle of segmentary unilineal descent as a model belonging to the realm of ideas rather than a scheme which could be derived from the direct observation of ethnographic facts on the ground.

So where have we got to? Although, in detail, I disagree with nearly all the arguments of all the individual anthropologists whom I have so far named, the position which I seek to expound as my own owes something to all of them. What then do I want to preserve?

First there is the idea of anthropology itself, which rests on a belief that, despite all our reiterated diversities, there is some real sense in which mankind is a unity deserving study as such. But the unity of man is a cultural idea rather than an objective fact and a very recent idea at that. It deserves more attention, and in my next chapter I shall examine how it came into being.

Secondly there is a negative proposition. Anthropologists of my sort are not counterfeit historians who devote their energies to the reconstruction of a past which we cannot possibly know.

Further to that I am not an historicist. I do not believe in the existence of laws of historical development which will help us either to explain or reconstruct the past or to predict the future. I am interested in the details rather than the generalities of the diversity of human culture but I do not consider that these details are, in any discoverable sense, causally determined. In history, what happens next is like the next move in a cosmic game of chess; the possibilities are delimited by the rules of the game and by the moves that have been made previously by other players in other places but what actually happens is not 'determined' or 'predictable'.

It follows that I consider 'development anthropology' a kind of neo-colonialism. On the other hand I have a cautious, anti-theoretical, respect for archaeology.

It is true that just as we cannot know what will happen in the future, except in regard to such certainties as 'one hundred years from now all readers of this book are likely to be dead', so also we cannot reconstruct the past by any process of rational argument. But archaeology is not all speculation.

Archaeologists are able to demonstrate the historical occurrence of a very small number of isolated, usually uninteresting, events. What is more important from my point of view is that they can often demonstrate that particular exercises in conjectural history are invalid; but they cannot do more than that.

Archaeology throws up endless fascinating puzzles: What were the historical circumstances surrounding the downfall of Minoan Crete? What is the significance of the alignments of the menhirs at Carnac? Who were the builders of Stonehenge and how was it used? The carefully argued imaginative speculations which are offered as answers to such questions are often very persuasive but in the last analysis they are always plausible guesses rather than prehistory, science fiction rather than science, though not necessarily any the worse for that.

From my social anthropological viewpoint the great merit of the archaeologists is their role as debunkers of anthropological speculation. No matter what we do 99·9 per cent of prehistory is irretrievably lost and we must put up with that fact, but interestingly enough, the remaining 0·1 per cent of the past which remains accessible through the skills and ingenuity of the excavators is usually quite sufficient to show up the total inadequacy of all anthropological dabblers in conjectural history.

Here are two examples of this debunking process:

1. Despite all the grand theorizing, initiated by Marx, elaborated by Wittfogel, and only recently refurbished by Harris, concerning the key role which irrigation agriculture is supposed to have played in 'the emergence of unchanging agromanagerial despotisms', the earliest large-scale irrigation system so far discovered by the archaeologists has turned up in Highland New Guinea. It dates from around 7000 BC and there is no evidence at all that either then or at any subsequent date was it associated with a large-scale political hegemony.[12]

2. It has repeatedly been asserted by all manner of sociologically-minded anthropologists, including both Malinowski and Lévi-Strauss, that the incest taboo lies at the very base of human society and that no social system could possibly survive which tolerated the marriage of brothers and sisters on any substantial scale. But the chance survival of papyrus records from very detailed census returns made in Roman Egypt every few years during the first two centuries of the Christian era has now demonstrated conclusively that marriages between full siblings were an entirely normal occurrence among ordinary members of the farming class. Since the Romans disapproved of such 'immorality' it seems likely that the practice had been current in Egypt since time immemorial.[13]

For me the fascination of anthropology lies precisely there. There are no 'laws' of historical process; there are no 'laws' of sociological probability. The fundamental characteristic of human culture is its endless diversity. It is not a chaotic diversity but it is not a predestined diversity either. Anthropologists who imagine that, by the exercise of reason, they can reduce the observations of the ethnographers to a nomothetic natural science are wasting their time.

This brings me to the third dogma in my personal position. Social anthropology is not, and should not aim to be, a 'science' in the natural science sense. If anything it is a form of art.

In any genuine science the only assertions which are of interest are those which are potentially open to refutation. Most of the propositions which are put forward by both social anthropologists and cultural anthropologists are not of this refutable kind at all. When they are, they are immediately refuted. During the hundred years of their existence academic anthropologists have not discovered a single universally valid truth concerning either human culture or human society other than those which are treated as axioms: e.g. that all men have language.

But if the findings of anthropology do not have the truth status of either history or science do they have any validity at all? Validity seems to me the wrong word. Social anthropologists should not see themselves as seekers after objective truth; their purpose is to gain insight into other people's behaviour, or, for that matter, into their own. 'Insight' may seem a very vague concept but it is one which we admire in other contexts; it is the quality of deep understanding which, as critics, we attribute to those whom we regard as *great* artists, dramatists, novelists, composers; it is the difference between fully understanding the nuances of a language and simply knowing the dictionary glosses of the individual words.

Evans-Pritchard came close to the core of the matter when he wrote:

I am not denying that the semantic difficulties in translation are very great. They are considerable enough between, shall we say, French and English; but when some primitive language has to be rendered into our own tongue they are, for obvious reasons, much more formidable. They are in fact the major problem we are confronted with in the subject we are discussing. . . .[14]

'The subject we are discussing' in this case was the anthropological study of religion but it could just as well have been the data of social anthropology in general.

The social anthropologist in the field devotes his efforts to trying to understand, not just the spoken language of the people with whom he interacts, but their whole way of life. That, in itself, is a problem of translation, of finding categories in his own ways of thought which can be fitted to the complex of observed facts which he records. But that is only the beginning. Having, as he hopes, gained 'insight' into what he has observed, he then has the further task of translating that insight into a language which his readers, who have not shared his personal experience, might reasonably be expected to understand.

So that is where I stand. Social anthropologists are bad novelists rather than bad scientists. But I hold that the insights of the social anthropologist have a special quality because of the arena in which he characteristically exercises his artistic imagination. That arena is the living space of some quite small community of people who live together in circumstances where most of their day-to-day communications depend upon face-to-face interaction. This does not embrace the whole of human social life, still less does it embrace the whole of human history. But all human beings spend a great deal of their lives in contexts of this kind.

All human beings? The phrase comes easily off the tip of the tongue, but what does it really mean? So let us go on from there to consider the history of this grandiose idea.

2   The Unity of Man

I have already put a good deal of stress upon two contrasted aspects of what seems to me to be the central paradox of anthropology considered as an intellectual discipline. The first of these is that while anthropology purports to say things about man and humanity at large, anthropological practice has fairly consistently been concentrated upon the study of 'primitive' man rather than man as such. The second complementary point, which applies particularly to social anthropology in the British style, is the (usually unstated) claim that we can exemplify the ways of humanity in general by making a series of close studies of particular examples of very small-scale and usually quite exotic forms of social life. The present chapter gives further consideration to the first of these apparent inconsistencies.

The majority of contemporary social anthropologists regards the distinction between 'primitive' man and man in general as anachronistic and untenable, yet to the newcomer it must seem that their methods of research and the themes to which they devote most of their attention take this distinction for granted.

In so far as this is still true it is a hangover from history. When modern social anthropologists write about 'primitive' peoples it is for want of a better vocabulary; they could just as well be writing about 'other' peoples. In their own minds there is no implied derogation. But the issue is not simple. In the earlier academic anthropology of the colonial era, which was only beginning to lose its grip when I myself became involved in the subject, we can easily discern an implicit equation which reads:

civilized: primitive:: master: slave

This is now embarrassing. No contemporary anthropologist, social or other, would want to argue that people of different culture must on that account be automatically ranked in a hierarchy superior/inferior. And indeed, since social anthropology is centrally concerned with the diversity of culture, it would be quite absurd if it could somehow be inferred from what social anthropologists teach that cultural diversity is both politically and morally deplorable.

My purpose in this chapter is to give an historical perspective to the antithesis cultural diversity/human unity. Thereby I hope to provide moral justification for the non-egalitarian presuppositions of the methodology that is presented elsewhere in the book.

At the very end of *The Order of Things* Foucault makes the seemingly baffling observation that 'man is an invention of recent date and one perhaps nearing its end'. Even allowing for the contemporary French intellectual fashion which puts a premium on witty forms of oracular paradox this seems a bit far out. What could Foucault mean?

Perhaps we can get some clue by considering a much earlier remark by another French intellectual, Joseph de Maistre, who was commenting, as an aristocratic refugee, upon recent developments in revolutionary France. The date is 1797:

I have seen in my time Frenchmen, Italians and Russians. I even know, thanks to Montesquieu, that one may be a Persian, but as for Man, I declare that I have never met him in my life; if he exists it is without my knowledge.[1]

De Maistre is saying that there is surely a contradiction between the revolutionary dogma that all men are born equal and the observed fact of cultural diversity. Foucault's comment is even more radical; he is challenging the very root of the Western twentieth-century liberal ethic of tolerance and individualism.

The United Nations Declaration of Human Rights takes it for granted not merely that all individual men are members of a single animal species, *Homo sapiens*, but that this biological fact carries with it moral implications. The species is presumed to be so homogeneous that every individual can be treated as the equivalent of every other. Hence the words man, mankind, humanity have come to be treated as interchangeable synonyms. Foucault's claim is that the very idea of such homogeneity is a very recent notion generated in, and appropriate to, the special political climate of Europe in the late-eighteenth century. This idea may now be on the way out.

I find this an intriguing proposition. Let us see where it takes us.

The potential ramifications of such a theme could be vast so let me start somewhere in the middle. I shall assume that the zoological species *Homo sapiens* is indeed a unity in the sense that *in the hypothetical absence of all cultural restraints* interbreeding between the members of any randomly selected human population of randomly selected individuals would be random, just as it would be in a randomly selected pack of mongrel dogs provided always that particular individual dogs were prevented from asserting dominance over their neighbours.

Dogs, like men, can look very different but when it comes to sex they all know that they are members of one species and they are not culturally inhibited from taking appropriate action. Dogs are polymorphic in appearance because they have been made to look different by selective breeding controlled by their human masters. Human beings are comparably polymorphic because, in the remote past, relatively isolated, relatively small breeding populations were selectively adapted to fit in with very different environmental situations. But all men, like all dogs, remain a single species.

But as we all know, in all practical situations, the interbreeding of domesticated men, like the interbreeding of domesticated dogs, is very far from random. Because of their cultural inhibitions all men everywhere behave *as if* they were members of many different species.

Once that is recognized it becomes quite obvious that the concept of man as a mythical universal being, born free and equal, which is today so popular among intellectuals and slogan-spouting politicians in all parts of the world is not shared by humanity at large. For the ordinary individual the concept man, or its local equivalent, refers to 'people like us' and the extent of such a category is often very narrowly restricted. It follows from this that there has never been, and never could be, an empirical human society of other than miniscule size in which all the individuals were, even approximately, 'equal', other perhaps than in the theological sense of 'equal before God'.

But the fact that we should now have come to believe that such a society might be both possible and desirable is certainly interesting.

My theme then is the dialectic between (a) the fact of the unity of man as a species, (b) the fact of the disunity of man as a social being, and (c) the mixed up ideology of equality and inequality.

First of all let me emphasize our common experience that most human relationships are asymmetrical.

Within the domestic household, where the triggered social

responses of the adult human being are first generated, perfect symmetry only occurs in the unusual relationship that may develop between identical twins. The normal dyadic pairs which are represented by the category oppositions husband/wife, parent/child, elder sibling/younger sibling, brother/sister, are always asymmetrical and can never function as relationships of completely balanced reciprocity. Hierarchy is not necessarily involved but individuals of opposite sex or different age status can never be socially identical except by some cultural contrivance as when the King of England is a Queen!

Likewise in the wider society of the modern industrial world most relationships are of the asymmetrical hierarchical type: employer/employee, teacher/pupil, doctor/patient and so on. Almost the only relationships which are presumed to entail symmetry and equality are those which we slot under the labels 'friendship' and 'enmity'.

In the kinds of society which anthropologists usually study, where kinship links of one kind or another ramify throughout the individual's social world, this contrast is often explicit. The opposition between 'consanguinity' and 'affinity', that is between relationships based on ties of filiation as against relationships based on ties of marriage, frequently matches the contrast between asymmetrical hierarchy and symmetrical equality. The prototype model for both friendship and hostility is then provided by affinity. 'We marry our enemies.' My brother-in-law is *either* my bond friend *or* my mortal foe.

This is not a general law. Sometimes the relation between brothers-in-law is asymmetrical like that between elder brother and younger brother and sometimes affinity itself is asymmetrical so that the categories 'wife-givers' and 'wife-takers' are distinct; but these are technical matters which lie outside the scope of the present discussion.

But to come back to enmity. While the friend of today may become the foe of tomorrow and the friend of the day after that, there is another fundamental category opposition which lumps friends and foes together as 'people like us' in contrast to strangers who are 'people not like us'; indeed they are not really *people* at all! There may be times when you feel entitled to exterminate strangers but strangers do not engage in quarrels, nor do they intermarry. Correspondingly, when we quarrel with potential friends, we still recognize them as 'people like us', both sides will conform to the same rules of the game. In sharp contrast, in wars of conquest and extermination against total strangers, there are no rules of the game. Strangers do not rate as human beings at all.

The relevance of these observations about the varieties of symmetry and asymmetry, social solidarity, subordination and hostility will become apparent as we proceed.

Cutting a whole sequence of further corners I shall now take it for granted that the total process by which we habitually segment and classify the things in the external world and recognize them as belonging to species entities originates in an introspective self-awareness that 'I' can be distinguished from 'my body'. This Cartesian illusion is directly linked with the universal belief that 'we' (people like us) can be distinguished from 'they' (people who are like us in external form but not like us in their inner essence). The central persisting human problem is not just 'Who am I?' but 'Who are we?'

We of course are *men*. But in what sense are we men? Where is the boundary between man and non-man? Let us review some of the facets of this particular strand in the history of ideas.

Pre-Renaissance views of man

All human societies, great or small, elaborate or simple, have
their traditional histories. Whether true or false or just part
true, part false, all such stories function as myths of origin, as
charters for human existence; they explain to the initiate or
to the newcomer how 'we' began and how 'we' came to be
where we now are.

Mytho-history of this kind provides a cosmological
setting for the time and space of ordinary experience but, in
addition, by exhibiting the contrast of possibilities, it offers a
rationale for the complex rules and conventions which
characterize 'our' particular way of doing things. In some
cases the corpus of story may imply a whole hierarchy of
discriminations: 'we' are distinguished from 'others', friends
from foes, recognized neighbours from unrecognized
strangers, gods from men, men from animals, 'real' animals
from monsters, and so on. The Christian Bible with its
progression from a wholly imaginary Garden of Eden to an
authentically historical Roman Empire by way of a
geographically very mixed up Land of Egypt and Land of
Canaan is prototypical of a species of origin saga which can
be encountered in all parts of the world among all kinds of
people. There is no clear-cut distinction between the
plausible and the fantastic. The topographical environment
is of great significance for the story but it is not ordered in a
straightforward way according to the canons of empirical
geography and empirical zoology.

In such cosmologies the concept of man emerges only
indirectly. 'We' must be credited with primal parents, a first
father and a first mother, who were mortal like us, who
procreated children like us, who, like us, were different from

other animals and other beings, both real and imaginary. But this egocentric/ethnocentric viewpoint generates a very restricted conception of what man is. There are a vast variety of natural human languages which contain no word for man other than the tribal name by which the people in question identify themselves.

The corollary of this position is that whatever we are not, that is what the others are. It is thus characteristic of traditional mytho-history that the real world of experience is surrounded on all sides by another world of the imagination which is inhabited by superhuman gods on the one hand and by sub-human unnatural monsters on the other: dog-headed men, men with tails, Amazonian women, cannibals, giants.

With the coming of literacy and the eventual separation of secular interests from religion, the world corpus of mytho-history has served as a quarry from which many different kinds of specialized literature have been extracted, poetry and drama especially. But it is not only the artists and the entertainers who have recapitulated, for their own purposes, the fabulous elements in primitive tradition; the academic writers, the learned purveyors of supposedly factual knowledge, have done just the same. Surviving materials from the classical world of Greece and Rome, from medieval China, from Arabia, and from Renaissance Europe offer many examples of this process.

So long as the traveller historians and geographers, such as Herodotus and Pliny the Elder, Chau Ju-Kwa and Ibn Batuta, Friar Odoric and Marco Polo, are writing as eye-witness observers, most of what they report is entirely factual and authentic. But as soon as they move to hearsay they lapse immediately into the purely fantastic, and the stuff of which their fantasies are constructed is lifted direct from mythology. Thus Marco Polo confidently assures us that the Andaman Islands were inhabited by dog-headed cannibals, while the Amazon women, whom he reported as living on an island near Socotra, turn up again, in identical form, in Columbus' report on his second voyage to the West Indies, only this time they are inhabitants of Martinique.

Dog-headed cannibals were especially popular. An alleged eye-witness account of the Mongol invaders of Hungary in 1240 AD provides gruesome details of their combination of sexual and dietary depravity. It would seem that in Cappadocea they were even converted to Christianity for, in that region, St Christopher is often depicted with a dog's head. But the case of Columbus is especially relevant to my theme.

The Greeks and the Arabs and the Chinese developed an extensive, and on the whole remarkably accurate, body of information concerning the geography and ethnography of 'the known world'. But though the extent of what was thus known was very great it was not felt to be unbounded. There was always the possibility that there might be other places, beyond the limits of the known, which were inhabited by the unnatural monsters of fable. Consequently, in classical and medieval times, there was no radical inconsistency between description based on the accurate observation of empirical reality and continued belief in a world of fable, inhabited by otherworld monsters. But once it was understood that Europeans might hope to reach the fabled East by travelling West, then explorers could reasonably hope that before very long they would have mapped the whole surface of the globe.

This is crucial to my theme because the concept of the unity of mankind could only become a fully meaningful idea when it became plausible to suppose that there was no hitherto undiscovered, unmapped, corner of the world where man-like but sub-human creatures might still survive.

It has been a slow business. The editors of tabloid newspapers are still prepared to finance expeditions to search for the *yeti*, the Abominable Snowman of the Himalayas. As late as 1942 I was myself assured most positively, by an otherwise sane Englishman, that, in an inaccessible valley just the other side of a visible range of mountains, he himself had encountered men with tails.

The development of systematic geography has provided an unhealthy climate for the survival of mythological anomalies but this has in no way frustrated the human imagination; the world of fable has simply been transferred to outer space. Science fiction has taken over the fantasy-forming role of traditional mythology.

But this is all very recent. In my youth I could read Jules Verne and H. G. Wells who took their hero explorers to the moon and to the depths of the ocean, but the imaginary worlds of Rider Haggard and Conan Doyle were still located here on earth in unmapped corners of Africa and South America.

In this context the first reactions of Europeans to the reality of the native inhabitants of the Americas is of particular interest, for here, in a very explicit sense, experience and fantasy were brought face to face.

As it so happens, Columbus' personal reactions can be reconstructed in some detail from documentary evidence.

He first noted that the Caribs were ordinary human beings and not monsters. He did not register much surprise at this important discovery, but it needs to be borne in mind that he supposed that he had reached islands near the eastern shores of Asia rather than a land mass inaccessible to the descendents of Noah!

Having commented upon the gentleness and generosity of the Caribs, he immediately reflected upon their vulnerability and upon how easily they might be enslaved. But then, within a very short while, fantasy reasserted itself and we find Columbus and his fellow travellers telling stories about other islands, as yet unvisited, inhabited by tailed men, cannibals, Amazons.

Among untravelled Europeans fantasy remained dominant for more than a century. Nearly all the earliest printed illustrations of American Indians concentrated obsessively on the gory details of their supposed cannibalism. Indeed the word cannibal itself, like the name of Shakespeare's Caliban, is derived from *Carribales*, Columbus' name for the Caribs. In actual fact it is doubtful whether any of the Indians with whom Columbus had direct contact ever ate human flesh. The illustrations, though mostly absurd, were based on later and more authentic accounts of cannibalism among the coastal peoples of Brazil.

The close association in European minds between savagery and cannibalism has recently been discussed by Arens (*The Man-Eating Myth*, 1979). It is an interesting topic but unfortunately this particular author abandons scholarship in the interests of sensationalism. Genuine cannibalism has certainly been a characteristic of human culture in many different parts of the world at many different periods of history; but it is also true that explorers, missionaries, and respected anthropologists have all, very frequently, given credence to stories about cannibalism which have no basis in any kind of evidence. The stories have arisen in the first place because cannibalism is a fairly standardized imaginary attribute of the bestial 'others', not just among Europeans but in the world at large.

By the time that Captain Cook was engaged in his voyages of exploration in the Pacific in the late-eighteenth century it was taken for granted that the inhabitants of the newly discovered islands would be men and not monsters, but cannibalism was still seen as somehow sub-human. Cook was thus greatly distressed and bewildered to learn that the New Zealand Maori, for whom he had developed a respectful admiration, ate their defeated enemies without compunction!

But let us get back to the sixteenth century.

From the very start of 'the expansion of Europe' the invaders tended to treat all the newly discovered peoples of Southern Africa and the Americas as less than fully human, a convenient doctrine which implied that they were legitimate objects for enslavement, exploitation and extermination. The criteria by which this 'sub-humanity' was defined deserve to be noted. Three captives put on exhibition by the English adventurer Sebastian Cabot in 1502 were described as 'clad in beasts' skins, eating raw meat, and speaking an unintelligible language'. Similar exhibits shown in France in 1506 were 'sooty in colour, black haired, possessing speech but no religion'.[2] In other words the essential parameters by which European Christians felt they could decide whether a particular other creature was, or was not, a human being – a 'person like us' – were then, as they still remain, *physical appearance*, *intelligence* (as manifested by language), *religion*.

The whole issue of the humanity or non-humanity of the American Indians was formally, but inconclusively, debated in tracts delivered to the University of Salamanca in 1550–1. Sepulveda justified the enslavement of the Indians on the grounds that they were the natural slaves mentioned in Book 1 of Aristotle's *Politics*; the Dominican Friar Las Casas admitted the frailty of the Indians but argued that they were all the more children of God owing to their very lack of capacity and skill, which still implies a sort of sub-humanity but of a different kind.

Not long afterwards the intrinsic intellectual inferiority of the American Indians was formally proclaimed by papal decree.

Montaigne

Montaigne's famous essay 'On Cannibals', written around 1579, adopts a stance which contrasts with both these points of view. It is of great significance for the subsequent history of anthropological thinking. In this case the cannibals were real, not imaginary. Montaigne claimed that he had obtained his information by careful interrogation of a 'plain simple fellow' who had lived for more than ten years in the French Huguenot colony which had been established around 1540 close to modern Rio de Janeiro.

Although Montaigne's ethnography is meticulous his purpose is philosophic rather than descriptive. His central thesis is that the only sense in which the people he describes are barbarous is that their customs are other than our own.

But *other than* does not mean *worse than*. On the contrary, Montaigne argues that the legal procedures common in the Europe of his day by which 'under the cloak of piety and religion . . . neighbours and fellow citizens [were allowed] to tear by rack and torture a body still full of feeling, to roast it by degrees and then give it to be trampled and eaten by dogs and swine' were a more horrible form of savagery than anything he had described as prevailing among the Brazilian cannibals. Elsewhere he remarks, 'we seem to have no other criterion for truth and reason than the type and kind of opinions and customs current in the land where we live. There we always see the perfect religion, the perfect political system, the perfect and most accomplished way of doing everything. These people [the Brazilian Indians] are wild [*sauvage*] in the same way as we say that fruits are wild, when nature has produced them by herself in her ordinary way . . . they are still very close to their original simplicity . . .

they are still governed by natural laws and very little corrupted by our own'.[3]

Here in embryo is not only the issue of moral relativity, about which I shall have more to say in my next chapter, but also the sentimental concept of the Noble Savage. Two centuries later this latter notion emerged fully fledged in the writing of the more romantic of Rousseau's imitators. It retains a surprising vitality in certain branches of radical anthropology even today.

The idea that the horrors of civilization represent a decline from a golden age of natural virtue in which ancestral man lived in an unspoiled Paradise, is an almost universal characteristic of myths of origin, the story of the expulsion of Adam and Eve from the Garden of Eden being a very typical example. But a new element in Montaigne's essay was its suggestion that the earthly paradise might be a still existing real place. The savages, whose natural nobility was compared favourably with our own, were not the imaginary inhabitants of another world, but, most emphatically, real people about whom Montaigne had received reliable information from an eye-witness observer.

Potentially at least, the concept of man was here greatly enlarged. And indeed it would seem that it was only at about this time, in the Europe of the late-sixteenth century, that a few thoughtful men first began to think seriously about the moral nature of mankind as a whole, as against the older, narrower concept of the moral nature of 'ourselves', God's chosen people, ranged against 'the others', the barbarians, who were only part men, unnatural monsters, beasts.

Savage and civilized: one species or many?

Of course grandiose ideas of this sort can never be said to be entirely new. In Aristotle's various treatises on the comparative physiology and classification of animals there is a consistent presumption that man is a single species. Apart from asserting that dwarfs are usually unintelligent, the author offers no comment on the morphological differences between human physical types.

But the implied unity of mankind seems to stem from indifference. Aristotle shows no interest in savages. In the *Politics* the existence of the city-state is taken for granted. All stateless individuals are presumed to be lawless vagabonds. Within the state, the *polis*, all the inhabitants are rated as men, in the sense that they are not monsters; but it is not assumed that, by virtue of being men, they are all of equal moral standing. On the contrary, some men are natural slaves; others are natural rulers.

Aristotle and his Athenian contemporaries were well aware that some barbarians were very different in physical appearance from themselves. Some of the Hippocratic authors took the 'Darwinian' view that this was 'caused by' adaptation to differences of climate and general ecological circumstance. Detailed illustrations on vase paintings and embossed metalwork show that the Greeks of this period were quite familiar with the physical appearance of African negroes. However, since representations of satyrs are often given negroid features, there is a suggestion that negroes were considered to be in some sense monstrous. But there is no evidence that the Greeks ever became seriously concerned with problems of ethnic classification; nor do they seem to have worried about the practical problem of how to distinguish between strange men and monsters.

But in Western Europe in the sixteenth century the situation was quite different. The size of the known world had, suddenly, been greatly enlarged. Overseas exploration and colonial settlement opened up vistas of fabulous riches; the existence of the barbarians could no longer just be taken for granted; they had to be fitted in and given their proper place in the ordinary man's picture of world geography. In this context it became highly relevant to ask a quite novel question: What precisely are the species limitations of mankind?

The debate was conducted on two fronts. The first was religious. Although most educated men were predisposed to believe that white-skinned, richly clothed Europeans like themselves must belong to a species altogether different from that of the dark-skinned, naked savages described by the traveller-ethnographers, there was the awkward fact that the book of Genesis declares that the whole of mankind is descended from Noah. And whatever the scholars of the sixteenth, seventeenth, and eighteenth centuries may have said or thought in private, there were very few who were prepared to come out into the open and publish opinions directly at variance with Holy Writ. The curse of Ham could be used as an excuse to justify the enslavement of African negroes but that did not make them members of an entirely different species; and anyway the American Indians were not even black!

The second front on which this issue was developed was part of a debate between philosophers, who were concerned with the moral nature of man at an abstract, idealist, level and the biologist-naturalists, who were concerned with the delimitation of man considered as a zoological species. The former were inclined to present their arguments within a mould of imaginary social history which assumed that, in his essence, man is a unity even though human societies are different; the latter were preoccupied with classification and were therefore predisposed to distinguish the varieties of mankind in the same way as they were accustomed to distinguish the varieties of animals, birds, plants and insects. Folk prejudice was on the side of the naturalists rather than of the philosophers.

During the seventeenth century and for long afterwards philosopher-humanists of Montaigne's colour remained a small minority; Shakespeare's Caliban, beast rather than human being, was the common man's stereotype of the newly discovered savages of Africa, America and the South Seas.

At the present time, in the context of the 1980s, politicians and academic anthropologists alike usually find it expedient to write and talk as if the psychic and species unity of mankind were a self-evident axiom. The scientists affirm as dogma that all existing men are members of one biological species, *Homo sapiens*, and all arguments about the significance or non-significance of racial variation in men are conducted within the framework established by that prior assumption.

But, in the past, the species unity of mankind has been hotly disputed. An early version of the alternative doctrine *polygeny*, according to which the global category consists of a set of quite separate races of quite distinct historical origin and wholly different psychological attributes was advanced by Paracelsus in 1520, but of much greater significance for the history of anthropology is the fact that, during a critical period between 1850 and 1870, polygeny was the dominant orthodoxy in scientific circles throughout Europe and America.

The theory is now in disrepute, but in side paths of the groves of Academe it still finds plenty of support. And it is still firmly embedded in the common man's common sense, a fact which unscrupulous politicians are all too eager to exploit. For obvious reasons it has special appeal for those who, on either political or temperamental grounds, feel a need to justify such institutions as chattel slavery, colonial domination, or any other of the cruder forms of economic exploitation.

By the same token the most vociferous upholders of *monogeny*, the thesis that all men are members of a single species, have often been deeply committed to political doctrines of social equality. This contemporary mix-up of science and emotion is unfortunate, for the scientific issues are much more complicated than the doctrinaire polemicists on either side are prepared to admit.

But religious and political prejudice and scientific obscurantism have been closely entangled throughout the whole history of this debate and the resulting jumble bears directly on my general theme.

Even when the discriminations of the zoologists began to be based on systematic classification rather than fantasy the criteria that were used to distinguish man from non-man remained very uncertain. Among orthodox men of learning the biblical axiom that species are fixed entities established by God at the Creation gradually became qualified by the doctrine of plenitude, the Great Chain of Being, which declared that God, as artist creator, would necessarily have created all possible creatures in all possible worlds, and that the creatures which we now know on earth are but a fraction of those which exist in the universe. But, so far as this world of common experience is concerned, all living creatures, including perhaps some that are now extinct, can be arranged in a continuous hierarchy, lesser to greater, with man at the summit, as stated in Genesis.

But if the total variety of creatures is so great and the

difference between one hypothetical created species and another so small, where is the boundary between man and non-man? What sort of creature stands immediately below true man in the hierarchical chain?

In 1677 Sir William Petty, an English scientist-scholar of distinction, declared that 'of man itself there seems to be several species to say nothing of Gyants and Pigmyes or of that sort of small men who have little speech and feed chiefly on fish',[4] which is all of a piece with Sir John Mandeville's wholly fictional fourteenth-century quest for 'diversities of folkys and diverse shap of man and beistis'.[5] In 1708 another English scientist, the anatomist Sir William Tyson, basing his demonstration on the dissection of an orang-utang, made the influential pronouncement that pygmies represent 'an intermediate link between Ape and Man',[6] a proposition later adopted by both Linnaeus and Rousseau.

Biblical anthropology

Arguments of this sort which confused the 'lower sorts of men' with the 'higher sorts of ape' were not simply exercises in increasingly refined scientific discrimination; they were closely meshed in with an ongoing dialectical debate, the original purpose of which had been to establish a synthesis between the theological doctrine of the Fall and the newly discovered facts of human geography.

The discovery of the Americas and of southern Africa had synchronized with the beginnings of European printing and, throughout the sixteenth century, the expansion in European understanding of world geography and world ethnology coincided with a tremendous spread of general literacy, which was in turn accompanied by the revived and intensive study of the Bible in vernacular languages.

This new learning posed many problems. How should one fit the discoveries of the explorers into the geographical and temporal dogmas of the book of Genesis? If the chronology of the Bible is correct how had the American Indians managed to get to where they are in the short interval since Noah's Flood? For that matter, how was the history of the Ancient World, as preserved in documents surviving from antiquity, which were now, for the first time, coming under critical scrutiny, to be made compatible with the divinely inspired, and therefore unquestionable, history of mankind as embodied in the Pentateuch?

The debate on these issues continued for several centuries and the proposed solutions were very varied, but all of them had the ultimate implication that only the civilized Christian Europeans deserved to be rated as true men in a fully human sense; all other 'men' being variously rated as sub-human animals, monsters, degenerate men, damned souls, or the product of a separate creation.

For example, writing in 1655, the French Calvinist Isaac de la Peyrère propounded his pre-Adamite heresy according to which there had been two separate creations. Only the Jews were descended from Adam and only the Jews had been contaminated with original sin as a consequence of Eve's disobedience. Noah's Flood had been confined to the Middle East. The rest of mankind, including the American Indians, were of quite separate and earlier stock, all members of which are, by their nature, lost in primeval savagery, except the Christians who have been redeemed by the grace of Christ and thus belong to God's Elect.

There were other ways of arriving at much the same conclusion but one logical consequence was that the non-biblical 'gentiles' and the 'savages' were lumped together as a kind of historical residue of 'first men'. Thus Vico[7] restricts himself to 'gentile' history (which includes that of the Greeks and Romans and North American Indians) but carefully avoids any challenge to the Old Testament. Likewise the celebrated ethnographic account of the Iroquois Indians, written by the Jesuit Père Lafitau early in the eighteenth century, carries the title *Moeurs des sauvages Amèriquains comparèes aux moeurs des premiers temps* but is largely concerned with parallels between the customs of the American Indians and those of the Greeks and Romans.

Somehow the doctrine of the Fall had been stood on its head. An optimistic theory of evolutionary progress was surreptitiously beginning to replace the pessimistic doctrine of universal decay. But the benefits of such progress were reserved for the white-skinned Christian Europeans.

The concept of Natural Man

The logic of this inversion deserves attention. Traditional mytho-history had simply polarized the time-bound, mortal existence of ourselves in This World of Imperfection against the timeless, immortal perfection of The Other World of Paradise. In this kind of mythological scheme This World and The Other World co-exist in different orders of time (e.g. as between waking time and dreaming time). But the stories in mytho-history necessarily have a linear structure in which one thing happens after another. As the stories are presented, the timeless Paradise is always placed at the beginning and the time-bound here-and-now at the end, though in some versions, as in Christianity, there is also a vision of an eschatological future when mankind, redeemed, will once again get back to the Paradisal beginning.

In a framework of this kind the processes of history are necessarily viewed as a decline from a Golden Age. But the picture can be modified if we insert into it the concept of a

primeval Natural Man, who lacks the corrupting appurten-
ances of modern civilization, and is, on that account, closer
to Paradise than ourselves.

Versions of this archaic theme appear in the eighteenth-
century philosophies of Vico, Rousseau and Lord
Monboddo, all of whom managed to invert the orthodox
Christian doctrine of cyclic redemption. In place of a fall
from grace which is ultimately to be followed by a return to
Paradise, we have the notion that mankind originally
evolved out of a sub-human stage of bestiality. The
beginnings of language and the beginnings of social
intercourse are man-made cultural inventions which mark
the beginnings of true humanity. In principle, just as society
was first invented by man, it could also be perfected by man;
but in practice, under the influence of civilization, the
intrinsic nobility of the first true men becomes corrupted.
Thus progress always overreaches itself and mankind falls
back into a new barbarism.

But because these social theorists recognized the possibility of a stage-by-stage perfectibility of human society,
they implicitly thought of culture as superimposed upon
nature. It was this that led them to postulate an original state
of affairs in which a hypothetical, pre-human, pre-cultural
Natural Man was a cow-like creature, without society and
without language, living in the wild in a Garden of Eden
forest.

The underlying thesis that the unity of man is natural
while the diversity of man in society is cultural is a still
prevalent orthodoxy among all Marxists and a qualified
orthodoxy among most contemporary anthropologists,
including myself, but it originally emerged, in the course of
the late-seventeenth and eighteenth centuries, as a dialectical
response to Hobbes' (1651) formula that, in the beginning,
man had been like Cain, a wanderer in the wilderness, whose

life was one of 'continual fear and danger of violent death . . . solitary, poor, nasty, brutish, and short'.

Vico and Rousseau simply took the biblical imagery one step further back to a pre-Adamite, non-rational, world of peace and innocence. The state of continual fear which Hobbes attributed to natural man *outside* society was, for Vico, a characteristic of emergent civilized man *inside* society, and this became the generative source for much of human culture.

Meanwhile Hobbes' low opinion of natural man as an individual was given a different twist by Locke (1690) who emphasized that not only is man outside society an amoral being but that the distinction between moral and amoral behaviour itself depends upon social conventions.

Locke supported his thesis concerning moral relativity by citing a whole string of entirely fanciful ethnographic horror stories such as: 'it is familiar among the Mingrelians, a people professing Christianity, to bury their children alive without scruple. There are places where they eat their own children. The Caribees were wont to geld their children on purpose to fat and eat them . . .'.[8]

The Great Chain of Being has here become a matter of moral variety rather than biological species variety, but it is quite plain where Locke would have wanted to place himself. It is his own culture which represents moral respectability; the amoral others are perceived as monstrous cannibals. The underlying ethic is that of the traditional folk mythology from which we started out.

Versions of Locke's doctrine of cultural relativity are still staunchly upheld by many professional anthropologists of high repute, though my demonstration that it incorporates the traditional proposition that the opposition 'we'/'they' is the equivalent of 'human being'/'monster' should serve as a warning. But the dilemma is more subtle than that.

From 1650 onwards, in partial imitation of Hobbes, a variety of authors managed in their different ways to transform the biblical thesis that civilization reflects a decline from a pristine state of grace into a cynical doctrine which declares that the observed condition of man in society has been superimposed by social restraints or cultural conditioning upon a pre-human condition of animality in which 'man' was a solitary brute devoid of any kind of natural humanity.

Whether you welcome this idea or view it with horror will depend upon who you are. Gramsci's reading of Marx according to which 'there does not exist an abstract fixed immutable human nature; . . . human nature is the totality of historically determined social relations'[9] is in line with this style of thinking; so also is Rousseau's earlier, portentous but shocking prediction that, because of human avarice, men would have to be 'forced to be free'.

Let us consider this paradox. It arises because the concept of the unity of man is being used in two quite different senses. On the one hand, unity is seen as *equivalence*. All human individuals are on a par, but each is separate from every other like the matches in a match box. Alternatively, unity is viewed as *social solidarity*. Here, in the ideal case, the network of social relations would embrace the whole of mankind: 'all men are brothers'. But the political objectives implicit in these two versions of humanity are diametrically opposed: liberal individualism on the one hand; socialist solidarity on the other. Populist theories of political democracy which suggest that meaningful forms of social organization can emerge from a principle of 'one man, one vote' fudge the issue. In effect, demagogy of this sort pretends that societies are indistinguishable from crowds. That is not how things are. And indeed the main task of the social anthropologist is to demonstrate just how fundamental is the difference between a social group and an unstructured crowd.

All actual human societies, as we can now observe them, whether they be large or small, complex or simple, are hierarchically ordered. The division of labour is always reflected in differentiation of status. Admittedly, ethnography presents us with a few (but very few) examples of value systems in which inequality of status is viewed as a moral evil; but these cases are so exceptional that they probably always represent transient states of society. The followers of a charismatically inspired prophet may, for a while, feel and act as if they were all equally members of God's elect, but if the community is to survive, the 'routinization of charisma', to use Weber's term, always recreates a hierarchically ordered social structure.

In the vast majority of cases hierarchical inequality is taken for granted as part of the natural order of things. And this is hardly surprising, for without hierarchy there can be no legitimacy, and without legitimacy there can be no enduring social order.

In a society in which egalitarian notions are taken seriously each individual sees himself as being personally directly inspired by the ultimate divine source of morality. My actions are their own justification. I recognize no human moral authority outside my existential self. There is no allocation of legitimacy to others. Human authority is then an evil in itself and the social relations which constitute the fabric of society are constantly being dissolved.

Hence all egalitarian doctrine is fundamentally millenarian, revolutionary and transitional. Despite the claims of the late Chairman Mao the notion of 'permanent revolution' is a contradiction in terms.

We know very little about the world history of such ideas and their dialectical development, but we do know a good deal about how things have gone in the main literate civilizations over the past four thousand years. We know that, in general, the *literati* became the bureaucratic agents of the established political order and that they always took it for granted that hierarchy is part of the natural order of things. The periodic appearance of literate philosophers who preach the equality of man is thus itself a kind of paradox. As has often been noted, such individuals very seldom practise what they preach.

The concept of political freedom, which is now so frequently bandied around by the coiners of political slogans, was, so far as we know, first developed in Athens in the fourth century BC where at least two-thirds of the population had the status of chattel slaves. Egalitarian Rousseau lived out his life as the spoilt plaything of eccentric aristocrats. Jefferson, whose eloquence on the theme of natural equality is constantly reiterated and was even written into the American Declaration of Independence, remained a slave owner to the end of his life. Marx spent his last thirty years in very comfortable middle-class circumstances in Highgate and was an employer of domestic servants.

What I am getting at is that, in these historical cases, egalitarian ideas were tied in with the presumption that the proposition 'all men are born equal' can be glossed 'all men (who are people like us) are born equal'. Equality does not extend to natural slaves or to those who are rated as infantile because of their seemingly intrinsic intellectual limitations.

The eighteenth-century revolutionaries in America and France coined some splendid slogans about 'government by the people for the people', 'no taxation without represen-tation', 'one man; one vote' and so on, but after some disastrous preliminary experiments with mob rule, they quickly settled for compromise; only the existing owners of property should be qualified to vote! To some extent it may be that things are now different, but then it could be that parliamentary democracy is no longer a truly viable form of political organization. Equality of voting rights certainly does not result in equality of power or the disappearance of hierarchy in government. Indeed, in Marxist régimes, despite a certain genuflexion to egalitarian slogans, *democracy* has become, quite blatantly, a brand name for despotic rule by a self-appointed oligarchy.

Prior to the eighteenth century the Europeans seem to have handled the ethnographic aspects of these dilemmas without much difficulty. In the early years of the Spanish and Portuguese colonial expansion the Church militant got itself into some considerable moral tangles, but these did not prove insuperable. The medieval Church had laid down categorical rules about the impropriety of Christians enslaving other Christians but these rules were waived when it became a matter of enslaving black Africans.

In their overseas colonies the Portuguese and the Spanish alike took vigorous steps to convert the local inhabitants to Christianity. To that extent at least they recognized, from the start, that these 'others' were 'men'; but they were only second-class men. As early as the middle of the fifteenth century, as part of a political deal with the King of Congo, the Portuguese actually managed to ordain a black African bishop. But the official church hierarchy strongly disapproved. No other African became a bishop until well on into the twentieth century![10]

In general, from 1450 onwards, non-European Christians were taught theology to a level at which they might function as parish priests, but they were not admitted to the religious orders such as the Jesuits and the Dominicans. When Goanese Christians complained of this discrimination they were told to start their own order, which they did very successfully. But they were still rated as 'other', a race apart.

Yet it would seem that, in the latter half of the eighteenth century, the movement of thought which generated the idealistic rhetoric of the American and French revolutions began to affect even the Roman Catholic Church. The boundary limitations of genuine mankind became uncertain. Sometime around 1745 Rome suddenly reversed its earlier policy and began, in theory if not always in practice, to treat all Catholics as members of the same species whatever their skin colour or cultural affiliation. Why this kind of change at this particular time?

Clearly there can be no simple answer to such a question, but we need to appreciate that, until the eighteenth century, the speculative moral philosophers who concerned themselves with such issues did not have to bother about the practical implications of their argument. Whoever the child-murdering Mingrelians might be they were certainly a long way away. They could be invoked to illustrate an argument, but they did not present a practical problem of social and political relationship.

But as communications improved and trade intensified under the aegis of industrial capitalism and European imperialism, it became ever more necessary to come to terms with the paradox: if 'all men are equal' only when 'men' means 'people like us', then where do the 'others' fit in? Most of us have not really solved that puzzle even today, but what did the question look like in the eighteenth century?

First of all it is important to realize that the anthropology on which the eighteenth-century philosopher-scientists relied reflected an indiscriminate mixture of biological and sociological concerns. Most of those who discussed human variety were talking about the differences in the physical appearance of human individuals, though they often mixed up characteristics which now seem to be plainly innate, such as skin colour, with characteristics which are plainly cultural, such as mode of dress. But other writers or perhaps even the same writers in other contexts, were concerned with institutional differences, varieties of law, of systems of government, of property relations, of forms of the family. It was because these two radically different approaches to a single subject matter, man, were barely distinguishable that the varieties of man came to be discussed under such vaguely defined labels as 'peoples', 'races', 'nations', 'tribes', and, more recently, 'cultures', 'language groups', 'speech communities', 'social formations'.

The parameters by which one such unit was distinguished from another varied according to the occasion but might include skin colour, stature, style of dress, morality, intelligence, language, religion, geographical locality and mode of subsistence, but there was always a clear presumption that the different kinds of criteria – physical, cultural, linguistic, regional, institutional, economic – were all coincident.

Linnaeus provided the model for all the rest. He listed the European and the African as two sub-species of *Homo sapiens*. The European was 'fair, sanguine, brawny; covered with close vestments; governed by laws'. The African was 'black, phlegmatic, relaxed; anoints himself with grease, governed by caprice'. We laugh? But open any British mass circulation newspaper any day of the week and you will find comments on the inhabitants of the Third World which rest on precisely such 'racial' discriminations as these.

Moreover although, with hindsight, such a classification appears scientifically absurd it is zoologically perfectly sensible. A modern bird-watcher's manual will distinguish varieties of finch not only by colour, size and other physical attributes, but also by psychological characteristics such as timidity and aggressiveness, as well as nest-building behaviour, feeding habits, sociability, seasonal and regional variation, and so on. If such discriminations are appropriate to birds, why should they be inappropriate in the case of men?

Until very recently the standard present-day answer to that question, at least among anthropologists, has been that man has culture and birds do not. It is a wholly unsatisfactory kind of answer. At the empirical level culture and nature cannot be discriminated in this way. And indeed I would argue that Linnaeus, in his role as classifying naturalist, did a better job at putting the varieties of mankind into their mutual relationships than did idealist philosophers like Rousseau and Jefferson.

For Linnaeus the varieties of men were like breeds of dog, different in their appearance, different in their manifest behaviour, but indifferently equal in their moral quality. I much prefer that kind of viewpoint to the egalitarian doctrine which declares that all men are equal but only if they accept *my* point of view.

Unfortunately it is the latter doctrine which dominates present-day thinking in the Western democracies, not only in the political parties of both the right and the left but also among most of you who are likely to be reading this book.

Let me return briefly to Foucault. If you read his book you will see that what he seems to have had in mind when he coined the phrase about man being 'an invention of recent date and one perhaps nearing its end' was something like this.

The unitary, all embracing, concept of man which is postulated by such expressions as 'Anthropology is the science of man' is really a by-product of the post-Cartesian attempt to objectify everything in the world, to view human relationships as commodities, to see everything as quantifiable and predictable and governed by simple laws of cause and effect. A concept of man, in this sense, only became

necessary when an objective, 'science of man' came to be
envisaged as a desirable and attainable possibility. In this
context Foucault argues that whereas economics, sociology,
demography and other mathematicized (statistical) social
studies are, despite their limitations, 'sciences', in the sense
envisaged, psycho-analysis, ethnology and linguistics should
be regarded as counter-sciences since they lead to a
dissolution of man considered as an objective entity.

I would like to believe that he is right though I notice with
regret that the academic professions of social and cultural
anthropology are in fact full of people who would like to
objectify 'man' by loading down their publications with
tables of statistics. Yet it is true that, although Foucault's
'counter-sciences', by repeatedly demonstrating the apparently endless variety of what is humanly possible, have
constantly served to enlarge the scope of 'us' at the expense
of 'other', they have, at the same time, ended up by making
the generality man so imprecise as to be almost meaningless.

Perhaps a future generation will come to recognize that
the most misguided, though well intentioned, feature of our
present age was that, having discovered by the methods of
genuine science that man is a single zoological species and
thus a unity in his *physical* nature, we tried, by political
coercion and propaganda, to impose on man, as cultural
moral being, a comparable sense of unity which contradicts
the very essence of our *human* nature.

3   Humanity and Animality

As I stated at the beginning of this book, the common thread that runs through the different chapters is the problem of continuity/discontinuity. The time and space of ordinary experience seem to be continuous. There is an oscillation between light and darkness but no particular moment of time when day becomes night or night day; as I walk across the landscape I may sometimes be on a hill top and sometimes in a valley bottom but at no point does the surface of the earth come to an end.

By contrast, the time and space of the man-made world of social events and human possessions is marked with discontinuities whichever way we look or feel or listen: 'at the third stroke it will be seven fifty-nine precisely . . . PIP . . . PIP . . . PIP,' says the voice on the radio clock. Our quest for order within disorder leads to fragmentation. Fences, gates, barriers of all kinds bar the way. We only feel emotionally comfortable when everything can be tidily sorted out according to categories. Is it a boy or a girl? Is he a child or an adult? Are you a Marxist or an anti-Marxist? Are you a man or a mouse?

In the past that last question has not always seemed quite as simple as it might now appear. But in a slightly different form the problem is still with us. If all men are human beings, why should we need two categories instead of one? Is our humanity in any way *different from* our animality?

Our classifications depend upon who we are. Botanists

will divide the world of plants into hundreds of thousands of different species; I find I can get along quite happily with a few dozen. But when it comes to the varieties of anthropology I get fussy, as you saw in Chapter 1. Some parts of our classifying schemes are essential. The species could not survive if men and women could not recognize that they were both alike as members of one species and different as individuals of opposite sex. Also we must recognize the difference between food and not-food and so on. But the methodology of modern laboratory science and of modern industry, whereby the first step in analysis always consists of breaking down continuous unity into innumerable separated discontinuities, certainly goes too far. We need to know how things are related, not just how they can be taken apart.

It is partly because of this distinction that, for the past fifty years, the physical anthropologists, who have by now become laboratory scientists *par excellence*, have barely been in communication with the various kinds of socio-cultural anthropologists. The physical anthropologists concern themselves with the history and distribution of the varieties of mankind considered as species and sub-species. Their methods are those of the anatomist and the geneticist. They treat the physical body of the human individual as a naturally existing unit separate from all others and proceed to take it to pieces.

Until quite recently the socio-cultural anthropologists have adopted a very similar stance. They too have assumed that there is something natural and self-evident about the human individual as a separate physical body, but then, in order to distinguish their own field of enquiry from that of the physical anthropologists, they have reified their special concept of culture to a point where we end up with the implicit definition: 'Culture is everything which concerns the life and behaviour of human beings which is *not* an aspect of human nature, as the physical anthropologists perceive it.'

Plainly this kind of polarized demarcation is absurd. Physical anthropologists and socio-cultural anthropologists have different fields of interest but their respective territories are not separated by an impenetrable wall; or at any rate they ought not to be.

Socio-cultural anthropologists do not need to be expert anatomists or geneticists or specialists in the biology of nutrition but they are likely to talk a lot of nonsense if they do not take account of what experts in such matters have been able to discover. Correspondingly studies in the biological aspects of human adaptation need to be supplemented by ethnographic and socio-cultural investigations of various kinds. But since the biologists operate within the quantitative framework of statistically based natural science, while the socio-cultural anthropologists mostly argue on the basis of intuition, communication between the two sides is very difficult.

In this chapter I shall not be attempting to show how this problem might be resolved. My purpose rather is to discuss the underlying issues in general terms and at a somewhat philosophic level. At one remove my purpose is also to show where my admiration for functionalist empiricism stops short and my interest in structuralist idealism begins.

The underlying themes have been spelled out already. What is the relationship between human nature and human culture? Is anthropology a science or an art? Do the protean variations of culture somehow reflect a principle of social evolution through adaptation to the environment which is directly analogous to the process of physical evolution that is postulated in the Darwin-Mendel theory of the 'survival of the fittest' through genetic natural selection? Should the social anthropologists abandon the pretence that they are natural scientists in disguise and think of themselves only as 'scientists' in Vico's sense – scholars in pursuit of understanding? In that case should they perhaps think of variations in human culture as expressions of permutations in the working of the human mind?

Almost all the alternative possibilities that are opened up by possible answers to such questions have quite recently been supported, sometimes with great passion, by anthropologists of international renown. I am not myself wholeheartedly committed to any of them but they deserve our attention.

In one form or another these issues, which are really all variations of the same issue, are of very long standing, but the style in which they are presented is liable to change very rapidly. Contemporary (and doubtless very temporary) fashion tends to represent the anthropology-as-science/anthropology-as-art opposition as the contrast between E. O. Wilson-style sociobiology and Lévi-Strauss-style structuralism. But the anthropological arguments presented in Wilson's *On Human Nature* (1978) are of such startling incompetence that, in those terms, a debate could never get started at all. On the other hand the cautiously scientific, but unsensational, studies of population geneticists such as Cavalli-Sforza are usually too technical to provide a basis for any dialogue with the intuitionists. So I will evade current controversy and take a step back into history.

The culture-as-an-aspect-of-nature/culture-as-an-aspect-of-mind antithesis has a respectable antiquity. Modern science, which is commonly held to have been given its philosophical base by Descartes, has nearly always presupposed precisely this kind of dualistic contrast between objective matter and introspective mind.

MIND	MATTER
unpredictable; governed by 'free will', 'chance', 'imagination'; responds only to sense perceptions	Predictable; governed by immutable 'laws of nature'

UNIVERSE	UNIVERSE
Modelled in the mind of the observer; open to manipulation by hypothesis	As it 'really exists out there'; inaccessible to human minds except as mediated through the human senses

HUMAN OBSERVER	THE STUFF HE OBSERVES
Capable of error and wilful deception	Incapable of either error or deception

Figure 3.1: *Dualistic (Cartesian) schema in which the human being is a privileged observer of a non-human universe*

Figure 3.1 is intended to represent Cartesian dualism in a schematic, highly simplified form. Contemporary scientific orthodoxy still operates, for the most part, within this framework. The scientific observer conceives of himself as a rational mind looking out through a plate-glass window on to an inaccessible 'nature'. This 'nature' is what is *really* there, not just what appears to be there. It is governed by discoverable mechanical laws which can be expressed in mathematical and chemical formulae. The model of the natural world which the scientific observer thus builds up in his mind is testable and 'true', but it is different from nature. The mind of the human observer is endowed with creative imagination; this allows the scientist not only to make discoveries about the laws of nature but to tamper with them and exploit them to his own advantage.

Now I doubt if any modern scientist really believes that 'mind' and 'matter' are distinguishable in this simple dualistic way; it is simply that the experimental research worker, in his laboratory, is bound, by the context of his work, to act *as if* he believed it. For if he did not assume that 'mind' is an exclusive property of the observer, he would have to suppose that the stuff he observes possesses the same qualities of imagination as he claims for himself. In that case nature would be capable of wilful deception and all scientific investigation would be a waste of time.

Now you can see that if a scientist of this kind tries to study man he is in difficulty. For he must then begin to assume that the object under investigation has the same characteristics as himself. This is immediately relevant to our problem.

Sociobiologists claim that they have a general theory about animal behaviour, and the category 'animal' includes 'man'. But the theory is a mechanistic one; the individual creature is genetically pre-programmed to act in the way it does; statistically speaking it has no choice; within a narrow range of variation, it always makes a predictable response to identifiable patterns of stimuli originating in the external environment.

But in that case what is the status of the sociobiologist himself? If he too is just an automaton driven by his genetic predispositions what can be the scientific value of his observations?

This is the converse of the main theme of Chapter 2. There the issue was: Can there be other creatures who resemble men in appearance, but are not true men, not really 'people like us'? Here we are concerned with the larger problem of the relationship between men as a class and other animals as a class. This question too has had a long history though it is only quite recently that it has become a precisely defined issue of zoological theory. But questions of this sort are not just matters of zoological taxonomy, they are also the necessary central problem for all religious systems and this is what brings them within the scope of social anthropology.

If, as human beings, we have moral duties both towards non-human living things, as the first chapter of Genesis suggests and the environmentalists believe, where do we draw the moral (as distinct from the zoological) line between the human and the non-human? For example, in Buddhist ideology the theory of the transmigration of souls implies that taking animal life in any fashion is a sin. But this doctrine is often coupled with another which denigrates the status of women as a class. Evil men may be reborn as sub-human animals, but virtuous men have at least the prospect that they may escape from the cycle of rebirths into the nirvana of final extinction. But the best that a virtuous woman can hope for is that she be reborn as a man. This is a long way from sociobiology, but we are back again at the problem of continuity/discontinuity.

The criteria for discrimination are very variable and when European writers of the eighteenth and nineteenth centuries at last began to realize (perhaps inadvisedly) that the word *religion* might be applied to other systems of thought besides Christianity this was one of the factors on which the classification of religions was based.

Totemism was low and primitive because men and animals are there represented as having a confused common origin. *Animism* was likewise low and primitive because it was said to imply that souls inhabit animals and trees just as they inhabit men. But Christianity was a high religion because it implies a clear-cut discontinuity between ethically conscious human beings, who have souls, and irrational beasts, who do not.

On this issue the debate between T. H. Huxley and Bishop Wilberforce at the British Association meeting of 1860 over the significance of Darwin's recently published *The Origin of*

Species has entered into our mythology. As is usual in such cases the myth seems to be somewhat remote from the historical facts but, for what it is worth, Wilberforce is supposed to have remarked that: 'Whatever certain people might believe he would not look at the monkeys in the Zoological Gardens as connected with his ancestors', to which Huxley replied: 'I would rather be descended from an ape than a bishop', which has merits as repartee but is hardly a contribution to science.

What was really said on that occasion is not on record but Wilberforce had just written a long review of Darwin's book in the *Quarterly Review* and from this it seems clear that the good Bishop was by no means the fundamentalist reactionary which he is commonly supposed to have been. He fully accepted the interpretation of fossils which had recently been put forward by Lyell and also the general interrelation of species in a Great Chain of Being. Where he differed from Darwin was mainly on the critical issue of evolution, i.e., the proposition that one species could change over time into another species, but his arguments on these matters were by no means obscurantist or naïve. Indeed a modern zoologist would probably find that he could accept almost as much of Wilberforce's argument as he could of Darwin's.

But although the myth misrepresents the historical Wilberforce, it correctly represents a very fundamental opposition between two styles of explanation of human behaviour.

It is something of an accident that the mythical protagonists of the two points of view should have come to be represented as Darwin and Huxley on the one side and Wilberforce on the other. The champions might equally well have been Epicurus and Lucretius ranged against St Paul.

What then is the crux? The materialism of Epicurus can be

summarized by saying that: 'The soul is a material body of fine parts and is distributed through the whole bodily structure . . . sense perception is a purely material process.' Substitute 'genetic endowment' for 'soul' in this specification and you have the essence of contemporary sociobiological doctrine. It follows logically from such a position that the difference between men and other animals is simply one of degree, a heightening or lessening of certain kinds of sensibility.

The contrasted metaphysics of the Christians requires us to believe that the human soul is a thing apart, which can exist independently of the human body. The body is no more than a temporary earthly frame for a separate special creation; it is the soul rather than the body which is endowed with intelligence, sense perception and moral judgement.

More crudely the materialist Epicurean approach implies that we are different from other animals because of our education. Each individual man starts out as an animal with a potential (genetic predisposition) for acquiring culture; we become civilized human beings by virtue of our training; our moral judgements derives from that training. All of which is, as you will appreciate by now, the strictly orthodox view propounded in most standard textbooks of cultural anthropology.

The opposite, orthodox Christian, doctrine is that man is different from the start and that moral judgements are absolute and known directly from divine inspiration.

Wilberforce saw very clearly that this was the issue and that evolutionism was damnable because it implied moral and cultural relativity. In his review article he cited, as counter to Darwin, a seventeenth-century commentary upon the twenty-first verse of the third chapter of Genesis.

The original biblical text simply says that after the

expulsion from Paradise: 'Unto Adam also and his wife did the Lord God make coats of skins and clothed them.'[1] The commentator sees this as a housing of man's immortal human soul in an animal body and proceeds as follows:

> And of a truth vile Epicurism and Sensuality will make the soul of man so degenerate and blinde, that he will not only be content to slide into brutish immorality, but please himself of this very opinion that he is a real Brute already, an Ape, Satyre, Baboon; and that the best of men are no better, saving that civilising of them and industrious education has made them appear in a more refined shape, and long inculcate precepts have been mistaken for connate Principles of Honesty and Natural Knowledge, otherwise there be no indespensible grounds of Religion and Virtue, but what has hapned to be taken up by overruling Custome. Which things, I dare say, are as easily confutable as any conclusion of Mathematicks is demonstrable. But as many as are thus sottish, let them enjoy their own wildness and ignorance, it is sufficient for a good man that he is conscious unto himself that he is more nobly descended, better bred and born, and more skilfully taught by the purged faculties of his own mind.[2]

Well there you have it in seventeenth-century language. Are we educated apes, or sons of God clothed in animal skins? Are our ethical values (the Principles of Honesty and Natural Knowledge) *connate*, that is 'known to us instinctively by virtue of our divine origins', or are they no more than 'long inculcate precepts' which depend simply on 'what has hapned to be taken up by overruling Custome'? Is morality nothing more than a set of cultural conventions?

The problem of moral relativity is still a burning issue both among anthropologists and among philosophers but I dare say that most readers of this book would like to situate themselves somewhere on the Epicurean side of the fence; so would I, but the intellectual difficulties which flow from that position are very great.

If you believe yourself to be simply an animal without an immortal soul but you also believe that you are capable of making moral judgements, you will need to ask yourself whether cats and mice and birds and insects are also capable of making moral judgements. And if you decide that they are not, then you are back where you started. What is the non-animal quality which men possess which other animals do not possess? What is it that distinguishes humanity from animality? Could Koko the gorilla become a Christian?[3]

Western philosophers of the seventeenth and eighteenth centuries who speculated on these matters usually emphasized two criteria:

1. Man has the faculty of speech;
2. Man is rational;

and they tended to see the one capacity as closely related to the other. They were also inclined to distinguish reason from imagination and to regard the latter as a sensual quality corresponding to the animal nature of man whereas intellect corresponded to his divine nature. Some writers even saw the transition from imagination to rationality as an evolutionary process; Vico and Rousseau, for example, both suggested that natural man would have spouted poetry before he acquired rational speech. In the same vein there has been a long-standing tendency to equate rationality with logic, and logic with mathematics.

Despite the salutary scepticism of David Hume this scholastic convention has survived right down to the present day and is perhaps best explained by saying that when intellectuals who have the mental habits of university professors are invited to specify the distinguishing criteria of human beings they end up by producing a self-image of themselves.

Detached objectivity in such matters is clearly very difficult but since it is quite evident that migrating birds and fish and even insects are often capable of solving the most intricate and unpredictable problems of solid geometry it hardly makes sense to argue that a purely mathematical rationality is an exclusively human characteristic.

All the same, the fact that we are *consciously* mathematical, that we *consciously* incorporate straight lines and rectangles and arcs of circles into our artifacts, that we measure things and reckon by numbers, does seem to be a very fundamental human characteristic which is of great importance for the way we organize our lives. And all the varieties of human kind that we know of do these things.

All the same, as against the scholars of the Enlightenment, my own general view is that it is precisely the non-rationality of our behaviour which marks us out as human beings.

Science, as it has developed right across the board since the end of the sixteenth century, has operated with the axiomatic assumption that events in the material world, out there, external to human minds, are governed by regularities which are so coherent and consistent that they can be treated as 'natural laws'. This all-embracing assumption is most improbable but it is justifiable since it never lets us down. When we investigate experimentally the 'stuff' of the world it never tells lies, it never changes the rules in the course of play. If we shoot a rocket to the moon and bring it back ten days later we can calculate before the start, within a matter of seconds and a few hundred yards, just how long it will take and where it will land, provided always that in the course of the proceedings there is no human error. Nature cannot make mistakes but human beings can and do.

Men do alter the rules in the course of play. Time and space 'in nature' are continuous; we make them discontinuous for our human social purposes, and we do so in a great variety of different ways. That is what the 'diversity of human culture' really amounts to; the variety of different ways which human beings choose to cut up the continuities of their animal experience.

But what has the arbitrariness of the *découpage* got to do with human fallibility? Let me take it slowly.

The question whether a capacity for error reflects our divine intelligence or is, as the theologians would have us believe, an invention of the flesh and the Devil is by no means a trivial issue of medieval scholasticism. It is precisely because human beings can 'change their minds' and 'tell lies' that if you try to apply the methods of orthodox science to the study of human behaviour you will nearly always get it wrong. But are we quite sure that this quality of unpredictability, which is, after all, only another name for 'free will', is really a human rather than an animal peculiarity? What about animals other than men?

As a general rule the strictly orthodox laboratory study of animal behaviour has always ignored this possibility. Psychological experiments of the rats-in-mazes kind are always set up in such a way that, even if the animals concerned had been capable of exercising individual judgement in such a way as to wreck the experiment, this fact would escape detection. It is assumed from the start that it is the experimenter rather than his subject matter who is in control of events. Accordingly, if anomalies appear in the results, this is attributed to defects in the experiment rather than to wilfulness on the part of the animals under investigation.

But there are other ways of studying animal behaviour and they have gradually become increasingly influential. The ethologists, some of whom prefer to call themselves socio-biologists, endeavour to observe their subjects in the wild, in circumstances where the gadgetry of scientific apparatus will have only minimal consequences for what is going on. And they pay special attention to the ways in which individual animals interact with one another to form social groups. In such circumstances the superficial similarities between animal behaviour and human behaviour sometimes become very marked.

A major difficulty here for an anthropologist is that the ethologists tend to describe their observations in language which takes the anthropomorphic analogy for granted. They regularly assert that the significance of an observed action is *symbolic* (rather than functional) and they start off with a basic assumption that emotions and attitudes are just as much observable characteristics as colours or structures.

Once it is conceded that non-human animals might have qualities of this sort the observer is challenged to interpret the alleged symbolism and the alleged symptoms of emotion and attitude. And this is what the ethologists and socio-biologists proceed to do, often with reckless lack of caution. The outcome is predetermined by the terminology. If a human observer sets out to interpret the 'emotions' of a rat what else can he do except say of himself: 'Now if I were that rat, how should I feel?' The issues here are complicated and I only have space to give a rough indication of where the difficulties lie.

The main difference between the sociobiologists and their ethological predecessors is that, whereas the latter were preoccupied with demonstrating the adaptive value of certain kinds of signalling behaviour in non-human animals, the former are much more dogmatic about the actual evolutionary mechanisms which have brought these (and many other) behavioural adaptations into existence.

Sociobiologists are liable to find themselves in confrontation with the cultural and social anthropologists because they are specially concerned with interactions (especially mating behaviour) between individual animals which are closely related biologically. They have this interest because such mating could affect the likelihood that an individual's genetic constitution would be reproduced in an individual of a later generation.

According to the sociobiologists, competition between individuals of the same species to achieve this end is what it is all about; the Mendelian modification of Darwin's dogma concerning 'the survival of the fittest' is made to explain almost everything.

The worry for the anthropologists is that some sociobiologists jump directly from their impressively careful observations of the mating behaviours of lions and deer and ostriches to sweeping assertions about the causal determinants of mating behaviour among men. This riles the anthropologists because theorizing about the rules governing mating between close kin has been a major anthropological preoccupation for well over a century. The anthropologists have not solved all their problems in this area but they feel, with some justification, that where human behaviour is concerned, most of the arguments now being put forward by the sociobiologists as if they were major scientific discoveries were effectively disposed of sometime around 1865.

The new-style sociobiologists, like the old-style ethologists, couch their arguments in highly anthropomorphic terms. It is true that when they use words like 'aggression' and 'altruism' (which they do a great deal) they make a pretence that they have somehow dissociated these terms from their human behavioural origins – but it is only a pretence. If an observer interprets a piece of animal behaviour as either aggressive or altruistic he is, in effect, saying: 'If that creature were a man I should describe his behaviour as aggressive or altruistic as the case may be.' As far as the humanity/animality issue is concerned, this begs the question.

And indeed the anthropomorphism of the sociobiologists goes much further than that since they regularly employ a language which derives directly from the ideology of twentieth-century capitalism: *investment, costs, benefits* are central elements in their vocabulary.

I do not want to get involved in the technicalities of such arguments but, for good or ill, the anthropomorphic style of sociobiological interpretation, together with its exaggerated insistence that virtually all patterns of animal behaviour (including those found in man) can be explained by evolutionary hypotheses, has lately served to reinforce and extend Darwin's original Epicurean thesis that the difference between man and other animals is simply one of degree, that there is no *natural* discontinuity.

Although Darwin himself published a book entitled *The Expression of Emotions in Man and Animals* most of his early anthropological followers ignored the possibility of a psychological bridge between the animal and the human. Physical man was supposed to have evolved from an ape by way of a 'missing link', but psychological evolution was discussed only within the defined limits of *Homo sapiens* where it was postulated that there had been a progressive development from the childhood of the race to its maturity.

As a consequence it has been possible, for over a century, to adopt two apparently quite contradictory positions simultaneously. Even those who have fully accepted the thesis that all varieties of animal, including man, had a common origin in remote geological time have still managed to believe that a clear-cut distinction may be drawn between the culture of man and the mechanistic responses which we can observe in the interaction processes of other animals.

The following quotation comes from Buettner-Janusch's authoritative textbook of physical anthropology published in 1966:

> Man, unlike a dog or a chimpanzee, can actively determine what meanings a vocal stimulus will have. This is the great difference between chimpanzees and men: men can arbitrarily impose signification upon vocalisations, chimpanzees cannot. A man can teach another man that a red light means 'stop'; a man can teach this to a chimpanzee; a chimpanzee cannot teach this to a man, and one chimpanzee cannot teach this to another.[4]

Although I myself believe that this statement is broadly true there are a number of serious research workers who now believe that it is false. The grounds for doubt are very varied but there are now several cases of chimpanzees, and at least one gorilla, who have first been taught to communicate with their human mentors in an apparently rational way by means of stereotyped signs invented by their teachers and have then gone on to use these signs grammatically, generating novel sentences as if the signs formed a genuine human language. Or so it is said. On the other hand there are well-informed sceptics who hold that, despite the honest intentions of the research workers, these expensively trained animals are just performing circus tricks.[5]

Both the evidence and its interpretation are clearly pretty shaky. The gap between the linguistic creativity of even the most intelligent ape and even the most backward of human beings is immense. But it is becoming increasingly difficult to maintain that the behavioural products of human imagination and of ape imagination are wholly different in kind.

On the other hand it has to be understood that, by the time that Washoe, Koko, and the rest of the humanized-ape fraternity have been endowed with elements of human culture in this drastic fashion, they have long since ceased to be ordinary apes. Although the process has not turned them into ordinary men they have, in some degree, become betwixt and between. Here, at least, an anthropomorphic jargon seems legitimate. Perhaps, from an ape point of view, they have acquired attributes of the supernatural! When the human teacher of the chimpanzee Nim Chimsky could no longer afford to continue his researches, Nim was returned to the community of zoo chimpanzees from which he had originally come. Nim immediately established complete domination over all his companions.

But Buettner-Janusch's formula, cited above, contains a further difficulty. 'Man can arbitrarily impose signification upon vocalisations' seems to imply that 'I' and 'my voice' are separate entities. But where is this 'I' located? If 'I' am not a metaphysical soul how should this 'I' be able to *choose* to say one thing rather than something else?

So we return to the original crux.

If Darwin was right when he argued that there is no fundamental discontinuity between man and the higher mammals in their mental faculties, and we accept, as surely we must, the *general* validity of the Darwinian theory of evolution and the connectedness of species, then where does morality come in? At what stage in the evolutionary process, and by what means, and to what end, does the possibility of making value judgements and exercising moral choices come into the picture?

The puzzle is fascinating and very probably irresolvable; but anthropologists need to remember that the roots of morality are also the roots of prejudice and intolerance. On that ground alone they should be on their guard against accepting any of the glib answers that have so far been put forward either by theologians or philosophers or biologists or even fellow anthropologists.

However my own opinion, for what it is worth, is that the possibility of making moral judgements is inextricably mixed up with the possession of language capability in quite a different form from that which has been shown to exist in experimental domesticated apes. And that takes us back to the issue of continuity/discontinuity between animality and humanity.

When I say we must accept 'the general outline of Darwinian theory' I do not mean that we must accept the dogma of gradualism which Darwin felt to be crucial but which is now becoming increasingly suspect. I fully recognize the scientific value of the sociobiologists' application of straight Darwinian doctrine to the study of animal behaviour in free, as distinct from laboratory, environments. But caution is needed. The gap between the human and the non-human is much wider than many sociobiologists would admit.

The value of the ethological study of apes, monkeys and baboons is what it tells us about apes, monkeys and baboons; only in very special circumstances, and in a very tentative way, should it be seen as a metaphorical alternative by means of which we can study man himself, as in a mirror.

The technical question of how far the biological continuity between man and other animals is already fully understood is complex. In genetic terms men and apes appear to be, in some respects, very similar, in other respects, very different. Quite apart from the hotly debated issue of language capability, the existing great apes are all creatures which can survive only in very limited numbers on specialized diets in specialized tropical conditions while the species *Homo* is just the reverse. It is constantly increasing in numbers and finding new ways to live off all kinds of foodstuffs in all kinds of environments. Most of this adaptability depends upon cultural invention but, in a limited fashion, *Homo* also seems to undergo quite rapid genetic adaptation to specialized local conditions.

The contrasted physical appearance of the different 'races' of man (stature, body shape, skin colour, hair-form etc.) originated as adaptations to life under varying climatic and dietary conditions as did the fact that resistance to particular diseases varies markedly in different populations. Some of these adaptations are probably quite recent, a matter of thousands rather than millions of years. Yet the latest genetic discoveries indicate that, on a different level, man is so close to the great apes that one researcher has seriously suggested that a man/chimpanzee hybrid might be a viable creature. Such a suggestion implies extreme stability.

Most palaeontologists have hitherto supposed that the nearest common ancestor of man and the modern great apes died out about 30 million years ago. That would imply a 60-million-year evolutionary gap between ourselves and 'our nearest zoological cousins'. Even if that figure were now to be drastically reduced orthodox interpretations of the fossil evidence together with orthodox evolutionary theory would require that the last generalized man/ape, the 'missing link' of the early Darwinian imagination, must have died out an exceedingly long time ago.

Yet it seems quite certain that our direct ancestors were walking around on two feet with an upright posture like our own at least four million years ago and no creature in the non-human line of descent seems ever to have done that. So perhaps it really all came about rather differently.

The early bipedal hominids were smaller than us so it is not surprising that they had smaller skulls, but there are no good grounds for supposing that men have gradually been

evolving into creatures of greater and greater intelligence.
Brain size and cleverness do not go together. And anyway,
even if we really understood how to measure intelligence,
that is not the point. We are looking for discontinuities.
From a socio-cultural point of view, the crucial issue is not
what our remote ancestors looked like, or the hypothetical
level of their IQ, but when or where or why or how they first
learned to talk. The short answer to that is that we don't
know.

Because they hold that the difference between a talking
creature and a non-talking creature reflects a quite
fundamental discontinuity, most social anthropologists
might be described as operationally anti-Darwinian!
Evolution evidently took place; how it took place is unclear;
but, since man has language and other creatures do not, man
is, after all, for all practical purposes, 'a separate creation'.

Why should social anthropologists hold that language
makes so much difference? My own answer to that difficult
question would be: Because language has the effect that
relationships, which among other creatures are generated by
inbuilt, genetically endowed, 'instincts' (as in the social
insects), or by individual stimulus/response mechanisms (as
in the mating behaviours of birds and mammals), are, in
man, reified as verbal concepts, and thus become matters
for group determination rather than individual determination.

That is a complicated formula but it contains the central
issue that keeps on cropping up in the debates between the
socio-cultural anthropologists and the sociobiologists. For
the latter, mating behaviour, which results in the perpetuation of the species, is the outcome of competitive strategies
of individual 'investment'. Whether the game is played out
'aggressively' or 'altruistically' or in any other way, it is
always the interests of individuals that are being served (or,

in some variations of the theory, the interests of another kind of biological entity, an 'aggregate gene pool').

In the language of sociobiology, 'kinship', outside the immediate bond of mother/infant and, perhaps, sibling/sibling, is a biological relationship which may be discovered by the research worker but which is not known to the actors in the scenario under observation.

But, in the language of social anthropology, 'kinship' has very little to do with biology; it refers rather to a widely ramifying pattern of *named* relationships which link together the individual members of a social system in a network. The naming is crucial, for not only does this make it possible to contrast one kind of relationship with another, it also allows the group as a collectivity to determine what the 'proper' behavioural concomitants of the relationship should be. The naming of relationships marks the beginnings of moral sanctions.

Language of course does other things besides that. It allows us to segment the external world of experience in all manner of arbitrary ways and to create artificial internal worlds to suit our convenience. Indeed it is impossible for us to imagine a social system operated by human beings which was not ordered by language; human culture, as we know it, could not have been invented by a society of deaf mutes.

But that comment shows anthropomorphic prejudice. Culture, in the sense of 'patterns of learned behaviour transmitted from generation to generation by learning rather than by genetic endowment', is a characteristic of many other species besides man. Bees and ants have extremely elaborate, highly organized, social systems which appear to get along without any concept-forming medium of communication which is even remotely similar to that of human language.

But I am making a different point. Human language is not just a tool by which we control other people and control the material world out there; it is also a device which allows us to formulate metaphysical concepts, and to recognize, at a conscious level, the binary oppositions which are basic to the structure of ordered thought.

A speechless ape presumably has some sort of feeling for the opposition 'I'/'Other', perhaps even for its expanded version 'We'/'They', but the still more grandiose 'Natural'/'Supernatural' ('Man'/'God') could only occur within a linguistic frame. If language is, in a certain sense, a necessary component of human reason (though ordinary languages are usually very inadequate for the purpose), it is also a necessary component of human art. This is really the heart of my thesis; the eighteenth-century philosophers said that true men differed from sub-men because they were rational philosophers rather than poets; the nineteenth-century positivists said that true men differed from sub-men because they were scientists rather than superstitious believers in magic; I am saying that men are men and not non-men because they have created artistic imagination which is bound up with the use of language and other forms of patterned but arbitrary expression, e.g. dancing and music. You might put it this way: We are human beings, not because we have souls but because we are able to conceive of the possibility that we might have souls.

Let us think about this. As I have just indicated, the anthropologists of Tylor's generation would have viewed such a suggestion with contempt. They were Darwinian gradualists who thought of human progress in terms of ever-increasing rationality. They believed that, in the fullness of time, as scientific thinking comes to supersede religious thinking, the whole category of the 'supernatural' will come to be recognized as illusory. Mythopoeic thinking will fade away because it will be seen to be, as Max Müller called it, 'a disease of language'.

Modern technology and scientific ingenuity has, in a certain sense, achieved this end, though not quite in the way that was expected. The supernatural performances of the characters of traditional mythology have become the natural real-life activities of twentieth-century space travellers; and this has occurred along with an apparent lessening of the gap between man and other animals. 'Conversations with a Gorilla' is not the title of a children's fairy-tale but of a supposedly scientific contribution to the *National Geographic Magazine*.

But in using the Comtean notion of progress from superstition to science as the mental counterpart of Darwin's physical progression from ape to man the Tylorians simply evaded the issue. For no one suggested that apes have the imagination to be superstitious! A fundamental discontinuity between human thinking and non-human thinking is already presupposed in the very arguments which were used to describe the imagined evolution from the one to the other.

But in any case it has been clearly apparent to all fieldworking anthropologists for at least sixty years that the various kinds of performance which have, in the past, been assigned to the categories 'magic', 'religion', 'magico-religious', are expressions of artistic creativity rather than misguided attempts to control the material world by mechanical means. And it is against the background of this kind of ethnographic experience that I am saying that the recognition of a distinction Natural/Supernatural (Real/Imaginary) is a basic marker of humanity.

But this is simply a roundabout way of reaffirming once again the fundamental significance of the fact that while men can use the apparatus of spoken language for 'thinking', other creatures cannot. In making this categorical assertion I am admitting that, as a social anthropologist, I really have very little to say that touches on the roots of our problem.

It is for the linguists rather than the anthropologists to tell us how language originated and how language is generated by human brains. But although the literature on these questions is very large and continually increasing, it is very clear that none of the specialists concerned know any of the answers.

Currently the most widely known (and also most widely criticized) theory on the subject is that of Noam Chomsky who has pointed out that, although children have to learn the meanings of individual words from their elders (which would make language a phenomenon of culture), they seem to know how to string words together so as to distinguish sense from nonsense long before they have acquired any substantial vocabulary.

Chomsky explains this phenomenon by suggesting that human individuals are *innately* endowed with a deep structure grammar of language. Extending these ideas, there have also been suggestions from socio-cultural anthropologists who have a leaning towards sociobiology, that, although the details of customs and moral rules and relational behaviours have to be learned afresh by each individual – they are matters of culture – we may already know in advance how to organize such conventions into structured patterns by virtue of a genetically endowed predisposition to become enculturated.

And why not? After all this is just what the theologians have been saying all along: We have had an innate knowledge of the difference between good and evil ever since Eve ate that apple in the Garden of Eden.

For my part, I find this revival of the ultra-metaphysical

doctrine of original sin under the guise of a genetically determined bio-grammar of cultural values, by colleagues who would clearly like to think of themselves as hard-boiled scientific rationalists, both amusing and disconcerting; but it points up the difficulties of the problem!

If there were any genuine cultural universals it could well be that they are universal because they are 'natural', i.e. a part of our genetic endowment. Many highly esteemed scholars have made suggestions of this sort. Freud proposed the Oedipus-complex as such a universal; Jungian psychologists have proposed various other kinds of 'archetype'; Lévi-Strauss has suggested the incest taboo; and so on. I am sceptical but, if there are such universals they are of a much more abstract structural kind. Here is a possible list which fits in with what I have been saying earlier:

1. In every human society, language and social be-haviour, in conjunction, serve to establish a category distinction between what is normal, natural, correct on the one hand and what is abnormal, supernatural, incorrect on the other. This distinction applies to the things that men make as well as to the actions which men perform. The distinction is arbitrary and it varies very greatly as we move across the map.

However, where technology is concerned, the nature of things out there, external to man, sets limits to what can be considered normal and correct. The 'correct' way of constructing a building could never be such that it would immediately fall down when it was completed. On the other hand 'correct' forms of action which approach the impossible may acquire aesthetic merit in the process. I am reliably assured that King's College Chapel in Cambridge, which has stood as steady as a rock for the past 450 years, could never be built today because the design would never be accepted under the safety limits of the building regulations!

2. There are all sorts of ways in which this correct/incorrect distinction may be expressed but I suspect that one of these is always geometrical. Correct forms are regular and simple, e.g. the English language usage by which *straight* is a metaphor for *honest* and *crooked* a metaphor for *dishonest*. The universal element here is that human beings use their resources of language and technology to *simplify* the world of experience so as to bring it under control. Nature is said to abhor a vacuum; human beings abhor complexity.

3. This moral valuation of the geometrically simple is a markedly human characteristic. Very simple geometrical forms exist in nature out there but most of them are ordinarily invisible to the naked eye. You need a very powerful microscope if you are to see the fundamental crystal structure of our environment.

And so also with living things other than man. When a man has cut down a bamboo it becomes a straight pole with a cylindrical hole down the middle, but that is not how it appears in the wild. Some birds' nests are hemispherical, but only on the inside; you must cut a honeycomb with a sharp knife if you want to see the accurate hexagons of its construction; the geometry of spiders' webs is astonishing but much less regular than it at first appears.

It is true that the non-human world of living things is packed with symmetries and topological transformations of smooth forms but the simplest shapes of all – regular straight lines, rectangles, triangles, circles, ellipses – hardly ever turn up except as the result of human intervention.

Yet such forms are entirely characteristic of human artifacts. Housing the world over is compounded of straight lines, right angles and segments of circles. Human machines everywhere are built up from mechanisms involving combinations of motion in a straight line and motion in a circle. The latest micro-chip technology has, at its heart, the simplest principle of all, the flip/flop, open/shut, give/take, reciprocity which, in one form or another, is encountered in all kinds of societies in all kinds of contexts everywhere.

As we shall see later the social anthropologist's view of society as a network of person-to-person relationships almost takes it for granted that all human interactions can be broken down into elements of binary exchange of this kind. What I am suggesting is that this use of ultra simple 'binary logic', which is tied in with the way we recognize speech sounds, is an inbuilt feature of our psychological make-up which distinguishes us as human beings.

What I have here described as the 'normality' which human beings regularly attribute to what seems to them simple, intelligible, logically ordered, in contradistinction to the 'abnormality' of disorderly unintelligibility, might, from a slightly different point of view, be seen as the opposition between the 'rational' and the 'emotional'.

At this point the whole argument not only takes us back to the eighteenth-century speculations about poetry versus reason, but begins to tie in with recent neurological discoveries concerning the workings of the two halves of the human brain which have been derived from experimentally induced conditions of aphasia.

Roughly speaking, plain, unemotional, ordered 'talking', which is heavily dependent upon our ability to recognize and encode binary discriminations (distinctive features in phonology and logical oppositions in argument), has been shown to be a function of the left hemisphere of the brain, while emotional responses, which are the consequence of reactions to sensory inputs from outside, are a function of the right hemisphere. The complete human being has to be able to combine both these kinds of mental function, the rational-semiotic-orderly on the one hand and the sensory-emotional-disorderly on the other. But most of us are frightened by our emotions so we like to pretend that rationality is *normal*.

Anyway, the implication of my argument, and of the neurological experiments to which I have referred, is that the functions of the left side of the brain have been developed in a very special way in the human species and that this specialization is reflected in the universals of human culture, including the general structure of language, all of which are reflections of the fact that the left side of the brain operates in binary logic. If that was all there was to it, we should simply be highly sophisticated digital computers. What makes us interesting is that we have a right side of the brain as well.

But if normal/abnormal equates with simple/complex, logical/illogical, intelligible/unintelligible, where does natural/supernatural fit in? If we move from the material world of technology and physical experience to the metaphysical world of moral ideas and the imagination we find that there is enormous discrepancy about what may be considered abnormal in different circumstances, but attitudes to the abnormal are always ambivalent. Normal is neutral; abnormal embraces both extremes, the morally good and the morally bad.

The ideas which in English are represented by the paired oppositions:

dirt : purity
sickness : holiness
power (potency) : impotence

have their approximate equivalents everywhere and serve to designate a focus of abnormality. Both components of each pair represent the extremes; normality lies somewhere in between. Thus *dirt* and *purity* are, in one sense, opposites but both are equally abnormal in relation to ordinary living. In relation to 'normality' they form a kind of triangle as in the −, 0, + scheme of my Introduction.

But it is not the objective facts that are abnormal, it is the circumstances in which they are observed. A room which is thoroughly comfortable when it is felt to be simply 'untidy' becomes uninhabitable as soon as it is perceived as 'dirty'. More critically, sexual activity, which is in itself a normal part of normal life, can suddenly become abnormal when it is classified as 'dirty'.

Lévi-Strauss' argument that the incest taboo marks the crucial bridge between nature and culture is untenable in the form in which it was originally propounded, since it is contradicted by the ethnographic evidence. Yet, at one remove, his thesis is correct. It is where culture sets limits on our sexual (reproductive) activity and where sexual capability sets limits on what is culturally possible, that our humanity and our animality interact. That is why the social anthropologists are justified in devoting such an inordinate amount of attention to the field of kinship.

Whatever is felt to be abnormal is a source of anxiety. Abnormalities which are recurrent and frequent become hedged about by cultural barriers and prohibitions which have the force of signals: 'Danger; keep out; don't touch!' Breach of such prohibitions constitutes the prototype of moral evil; the essence of sin is disobedience to a taboo.

Since the nature of the taboos varies between one society and another and even as between one situation and another within the same society, there is no particular action which is universally considered to be sinful in all circumstances: to kill a neighbour is a crime, to kill an enemy may be a duty.

Customary rules and conventions permeate the whole of social life. We are of necessity constantly breaking the rules and thereby committing sin, but some kinds of offence are more disturbing than others. Murder, sex, and sacrilege arouse emotion in a way that tax evasion does not. Such biases are not necessarily universal. In some societies breaches of conventions concerning dress and food and personal deference can arouse the most violent emotions; eleswhere such matters may be considered trivial. But sex, homicide, and religious cult are categories which we somehow *expect* to be hedged about by taboo, everywhere, always. Why?

I don't really know the answer though it seems a fair question. Sin and sex do somehow go together and this seems to tie in with the distinction I made much earlier on between the scientific view that man differs from other animals only in degree and the religious view that there is an essential difference in kind. Sex is an animal quality which must somehow be pushed on to the other side of the great divide.

The general effect of moral rules linked with the category distinction normal/abnormal is to provide us with a sense of social order. It establishes boundaries and compartments in an otherwise chaotic social living space. It provides us with a map; it tells us where we are and who we are. We are the prototype of normality; abnormality is the other.

What we need to know about 'the other', whether animal or human, is where he, she or it fits in.

Of animals, are they close or far, food or not-food, pets or vermin, domesticated slaves or savage monsters? Can we kill them with impunity, or only on set occasions in a special manner, or are they sacred and untouchable?

And likewise with human beings, we need to discriminate between close kin, more remote kin, friends, enemies and strangers. The categories in each case are artificial and social rather than self-evident, but they are necessary so that we can conduct our affairs in an orderly manner.

Within their own scale of operations all animals need to be able to impose an appearance of order upon their environment; they need to be able to discriminate favourable (normal) from unfavourable (abnormal) situations. Sexually dimorphic creatures must be able to discriminate members of their own species from other species, males from females, and so on. A peculiarity of human beings is the very weak degree to which we are endowed with 'natural' discriminating powers of this sort. In man, a culturally controlled sense of sin largely replaces the species-wide boundary-recognizing mechanisms found in other animals.

This leads to ambiguity of two kinds. On the one hand, as we saw in the last chapter, we are uncertain about the limits of our own species. On the other, we are all highly adept at creating socially defined sub-categories of man and then treating the members of the groups thus specified as if they belonged to quite different species from our own.

It cannot be said that there are any completely universal cultural devices by which we achieve these ends but certain kinds of taboo-loaded discrimination are very common. Some of these are familiar to readers of this book. For example, there is nearly always a critical distinction between the body which is naked and unadorned, which is animal, and the body adorned, which is human. There will then be taboos against appearing 'naked' in inappropriate situations, though just what counts as either naked or inappropriate varies greatly from place to place for no very obvious or logical reason. Covering the genitals, as in the Genesis story, is by no means an invariable symbol of modesty and minimal bodily adornment; and it would surely be very difficult to give an entirely rational explanation as to why it should be permissible to walk around in the nude on parts of Brighton beach but an offence against public decency to do so in Throgmorton Street.

But though one can find exceptions to all generalizations concerning taboo, it is broadly speaking the case that nearly all societies, either implicitly or explicitly, make the following three fundamental distinctions between humans and non-humans:

1. Men make use of fire not only to keep themselves warm but to process their food	Other animals do not
2. Men engage in sex relations with other human beings	Other animals do not
3. Men alter their 'natural' body form by painting or mutilating the body or by wearing clothes	Other animals do not

And, granted that much, 'We' then further discriminate ourselves from other men by elaborations of these same three distinctions:

1a. True men prepare their food as we do	Other men do not
2a. True men conform to our conventions regarding sex relations	Other men do not
3a. True men adorn their bodies as we do	Other men do not

In the outcome, food, sex and 'nakedness' are nearly everywhere the primary foci of taboo.

But further approximate generalizations are also possible. Quite apart from discriminations as to what is or is not permissible food and how it should be prepared ('edibility' in a strict nutritional sense is a very minor factor here), all human societies have precise rules about the circumstances in which men may *kill* other men and other animals. Such rules serve to distinguish further basic social categories: friends from enemies, domestic animals from wild beasts, and so on.

Likewise within any one human society, there are always very complex regulations, partly explicit, partly implicit, about the precise circumstances in which a sexual relationship between two individuals is to be deemed proper or improper, and this again serves to distinguish social categories: close relatives from distant relatives, wives from sisters, lords from commoners.

What does this explain? Well in a sense it does not explain anything; it is simply an elaborated gloss on my statement that homicide and sex are the expected loci of sin. But it ties in with my earlier discussion of ethology and my original Cartesian Figure 3.1, and with my assertion that we have a psychological need to perceive ourselves as normal and well regulated.

As I pointed out earlier, even those scientists who are most eager to assure us that the difference between man and other animals is only a matter of degree always conduct their experiments in a way which implies that the observer is quite different in kind from what he observes.

And so it is with the rest of us. We need to believe that we are different: that human beings are different from other animals, that 'we' are different from our enemies and even more different from total strangers. And we use moral evaluations about food and sex and homicide and dress and the 'proper' way of ordering a household as means of making such discriminations. We tend to favour simple geometrical shapes and sharply contrasted formal rules because they make it that much easier to distinguish right from wrong, normal from abnormal.

All of this adds up to a personal credo that we are not just specialized apes but a unique and peculiar species of our own. But in that credo the dogma that the culture and the nature of man are sharply and easily distinguishable, which has traditionally held a central position in the teaching of both cultural and social anthropology, has no part. If we are indeed a unique species then many of the behaviours which differentiate us from other animals are likely to be due to our genetic make-up rather than to cultural conditioning; but the difficulty is to know just what these animal-human characteristics might be.

Given our human circumstances, it is extremely difficult for any human observer to investigate a member of his own species as if he or she were a creature of nature, out there, on the other side of the plate glass. It is a worthwhile form of enquiry but, in this area, it is likely to take a very long time before the scientists can reach a consensus which will seem in the least convincing to non-scientists. Meanwhile, reckless generalizations based on variations of the Desmond Morris/E. O. Wilson doctrine that man is 'a real Brute already, an Ape, Satyre, Baboon' will not get us anywhere at all.

As I emphasized at the beginning, the issue is not just one of zoological taxonomy, it is a problem of ethics, and unless you *are* prepared to argue that Koko the gorilla might become a Christian, ethics concern rules which apply to human beings but not to non-human beings.

Academic anthropologists, and they are the majority, who still have their roots in nineteenth-century positivism, are inclined to underestimate the subtleties of such problems. The differences between human beings and other animals are complex; that is why they worry us. But if I have been able to persuade you that Bishop Wilberforce and Professor Chomsky are really saying the same thing, then those of you who are of rationalist or empiricist persuasion have at least got a measure of the difficulties that you face.

The elimination of metaphysics is not the simple matter that some humanist philosophers have supposed. The fact that we are simultaneously *both* animal *and* human poses a real problem as to how the two categories should be distinguished.

It is no doubt all to the good that we should rid ourselves of the delusion that our mortal bodies are inhabited by immortal souls, but, in claiming to be human beings, we are asserting our capacity for exercising moral choice and that implies moral responsibility. The responsibility is far reaching; whether we like it or not all living species on this earth are at our mercy and in our charge.

This is a situation which the tidy, randomized, and morally neutral competitive regularities of Darwinian evolutionary theory, which the sociobiologists treat as Holy Writ, did not take into account.

The whole argument is relevant for the theme of this book because, in the tradition of Durkheim, as against the materialist tradition of Marx, I myself view the varieties of human society as alternative systems of moral order rather than as a sequence of specialized adaptations to different economic circumstances.

4   My Kind of Anthropology

By this point some of my readers will be up in arms. What has all this grand talk about moral universals got to do with the micro-scale empirical sociology which I originally held up as the characteristic of my kind of social anthropology?

Actually, I have been slipping in quite a large amount of social anthropological theory while appearing to be discussing other things, though, at the grand scale level, I still have to justify my claim that a mechanical model of functionalist integration is to be preferred to an organic model. But before I take up that theme let me try to get closer to the ground. What is it that social anthropologists actually do?

What they are trying to do is to arrive at insights which are generally true of all humanity (including the anthropologists themselves) by observing very small-scale examples of human life. But how do they go about it?

There is a legend that Malinowski, in one of his more outrageous moments, once defined social anthropology as 'the study of man (embracing woman) while learning the local language with the help of a sleeping dictionary'. Certainly his own study of Trobriand kinship to which he gave the unnecessarily glamorous title of *The Sexual Life of Savages in North-Western Melanesia* gave the impression that that was the essence of the matter. In mocking fashion the fable puts stress on two outstanding characteristics of anthropological field research: a central concern with

kinship and marriage and an emphasis on gaining understanding through participant observation and the intimate,
first-hand, use of vernacular concepts. This chapter is
intended to justify those priorities.

So far I have been arguing that the essential subject matter
of all kinds of anthropology is the diversity of mankind, both
biological and cultural, while my own particular concern, as
a social anthropologist, is with moral (cultural) diversity
within a matrix of (approximate) species-wide biological
uniformity. But what does that entail in terms of anthropological practice?

Well first of all I must distance myself from the image that
is presented by nearly all introductory textbooks of cultural
anthropology. These books, suitably adorned with glossy
illustrations of exotic customs and part naked ladies,
discourse at large upon a variety of supposedly universal
characteristics of human culture which are then exemplified
by thumbnail sketches of ethnographic miscellanea derived
at third or fourth hand from a job lot of long ago
anthropological monographs. The tribal peoples concerned
are dotted around the map in quite arbitrary fashion; the
arbitrariness being emphasized by dot references on a world
map shown on the end covers of the book.

These samples of human oddity certainly exemplify
cultural diversity but the choice of pictures immediately
makes it obvious that the people who are to be discussed are
'primitives' who lack all the gadgetry of modern technology
and modern sanitation. Whatever the authors' texts may
say, the whole lay-out of such books implies that anthropology is essentially concerned with the lives of people who
are in some way inferior and/or deprived. We need to escape
from this traditional image of what anthropologists do, but
it is not easy.

It is virtually dogma among social anthropologists of my

sort that cultural otherness does not carry with it any necessary hierarchy of superiority/inferiority which can be appropriately labelled by such terms as 'primitive', 'backward', 'underdeveloped', 'childish', 'ignorant', 'simple', 'primeval', 'pre-literate', or whatever. My interest in the others arises because they are other, not because they are inferior. But in that case why study 'others' at all?

If social anthropologists are sincere when they say that their subject is a kind of micro-sociology and when they proclaim that they no longer feel themselves to be members of a culture/society which is intrinsically 'superior' to that of the people they are studying, why don't they study themselves? Why suffer the discomforts of living in a longhouse near the headwaters of the Amazon when versions of what you want to know are available for observation just down the road?

This is a sensitive and difficult question. Social anthropologists can and do study members of their own society and they have been doing so for a long time, though mostly they do not do it very well. Certainly, field research of this kind is not something which I would recommend for the inexperienced.

Surprising though it may seem, fieldwork in a cultural context of which you already have intimate first-hand experience seems to be much more difficult than fieldwork which is approached from the naïve viewpoint of a total stranger. When anthropologists study facets of their own society their vision seems to become distorted by prejudices which derive from private rather than public experience.

A case history will illustrate what I mean. Between 1934 and 1949 the Chinese scholars Lin Yueh-hwa, Martin C. Yang, Francis L. K. Hsu and Fei Hsiao-Tung, all of whom were professionally-trained social anthropologists who had learned their craft under the direct or indirect aegis of

Radcliffe-Brown and/or Malinowski, all published social anthropological accounts of Chinese communities. In only one of these cases does the fact that the anthropologist was, up to a point, studying members of his own society appear as in any way an advantage.

Lin was writing about his native village but he tried to evade the problems posed by autobiographical honesty by couching his story in the form of a novel. This artifice did not really work. It is true that, at a certain level, novelists and social anthropologists are engaged in the same kind of enterprise, but the techniques are different and, in general, they should not be mixed up.

Yang was also writing about his native village but he wrote about it at a distance when resident in New York. In the outcome the characters in his story are completely depersonalized. Indeed Yang's self-imposed anonymity reduces his book to a kind of caricature of a European ethnological description of a primitive tribe written around 1900.

Hsu's monograph suffers from the converse limitation; the author expressly claimed that he was studying members of his own society but, by the ordinary criteria used by social anthropologists, he was not doing anything of the sort.

His book is about ancestral worship in *West Town* which is presented as prototypical of that which prevails in Chinese culture as a whole. Hsu himself grew up in eastern China but his account is evidently a syncretic blend of what he learned as a child from personal experience and what he learned as an adult, several thousand miles away to the west, during fourteen months' fieldwork in the Yunnanese city of Tali-fu, where he was employed for a while as a teacher in a local missionary college.

The inhabitants of Tali-fu are mostly Min Chia, a population with a distinctive language of their own, and to

Hsu's personal dismay he was treated as a stranger: 'though regarded sympathetically, I was always an outsider, despite the fact that as far as physical appearance is concerned I seemed no different from those who made up the community'.[1] But Hsu was so anxious that 'West Town' should typify China as a whole that the Min Chia peculiarities of the local culture are hardly ever mentioned. This is a palpable distortion but the resulting stereotype picture is curiously static. The fieldwork was conducted during the period July 1941 – September 1943 but the book is written as if the culture of 'West Town' was timeless and entirely unaffected by the chaos of the surrounding political situation.

Hsu's account of 'West Town' may be compared with the explicit account of the Min Chia of Tali-fu published by C. P. Fitzgerald in 1941. Like Hsu, Fitzgerald had been a pupil of Malinowski, but he did not feel compelled to turn the Min Chia into Chinese. His research had been conducted in exactly the same locality as Hsu's but in the more peaceful conditions prevailing three years earlier. His book tells us far more about where the population of Tali-fu fits into the historical geography of Yunnan than does Hsu's more ambitious exercise. Hsu incidentally never mentions the existence of Fitzgerald's study.

These comments are not intended to challenge Hsu's competence as a social anthropologist (later on he was to become President of the American Anthropological Association), but to point up the fact that the understandable, and indeed laudible, desire on the part of some social anthropologists to study their own society is beset with hazards. Initial preconceptions are liable to prejudice the research in a way that does not affect the work of the naïve stranger.

But now a counter-example. Fei's volume was not only the earliest of the series; it was also the most Malinowskian in style and, most emphatically, by far the most successful. Fei was not a native of the community that he studied (the village of Kaihsienkung, in the Yangtze Delta, about 125 miles south-west of Shanghai), but he had grown up in the same district so that he was familiar with the nuances of the local dialect. Also it is clearly relevant that his sister, who was in charge of a local, government-sponsored, silk development project, was well-known to all the villagers. But when one learns that the whole project involved only two months of actual field research (July-August 1936), it becomes obvious that, in this case, the success of the enterprise must have been heavily dependent upon Fei's prior local knowledge. Incidentally, although Fei called his book *Peasant Life in China*, he made no pretence that the social system he described was typical for the whole country.

However the merit of Fei's book lies in its functionalist style. Like all the best work by social anthropologists it has at its core the very detailed study of the network of relationships operating within a single very small-scale community. Such studies do not, or should not, claim to be 'typical' of anything in particular. They are not intended to serve as illustrations of something more general. They are interesting in themselves. And yet the best of such monographs, despite the concentration upon a tiny range of human activity, will tell us more about the ordinary social behaviour of mankind than a whole shelfful of general textbooks labelled *Introduction to Cultural Anthropology*.

Despite my negative attitude towards the direct anthropological study of one's own society, I still hold that all the anthropologist's most important insights stem from introspection. The scholarly justification for studying 'others' rather than 'ourselves' is that, although we first perceive the others as exotic, we end up by recognizing in their 'peculiarities' a mirror of our own.

'We' – that is the readers of this book – conduct our daily affairs within a setting which most of us accept without question. Even a skeletal list of the fundamentally important matters which we thus take for granted would be very long. It would certainly include: the physical lay-out of the houses we live in and of the settlements of which they form a part; the general pattern of conventional procedures by which foodstuffs and other necessities of life are produced and distributed and finally consumed; the way children are brought up; the way tasks are allocated to different members of the household; the ideas we have about the nature of reality and of the cosmos, our sense of what is the proper way to behave towards kin and neighbours and persons in authority; the kinds of clothes and the styles of language which are appropriate to different occasions, etc.

The catalogue might be extended almost indefinitely, but the point that I want to emphasize is that, for the most part, these distinctive features of our own way of life are not of our own making. We do not live exactly as our parents lived but whatever we do now is only a modification of what was done before. It could hardly be otherwise. Very little of our public behaviour is innate; most of us have only very limited creative originality. We act as we do because, one way or another, we have learned from others that that is the way we ought to behave.

The whole system of things and people which surrounds us coerces us to be conformist; even if you want to be a social rebel you will still have to go about things in a conventional way if you are to gain recognition and not be rated as insane. Indeed, in social systems where the position of social rebels is not recognized, such as that of Soviet Russia, you are likely to be reckoned as insane anyway.

This will still be true even if you have been trained as an anthropologist. It is always exceedingly difficult to look at oneself within a familiar social setting without falling into conventional clichés. But social anthropological fieldwork is ordinarily conducted in unfamiliar social settings and, because the fieldworker is initially a stranger, he is not preconditioned to interact with those he studies in any particular predetermined way. This is a salutary experience. The anthropological fieldworker who eventually returns to the social setting of his homeland usually finds that it has become quite a different place. The bondage of our own cultural conventions has somehow been loosened up.

But what do social anthropologists actually do? I dare say they do many different things. I can only speak from personal experience. Fieldwork in this style is a very small-scale, private affair. The research 'team' is usually just a single individual, or perhaps a married couple, with maybe a local assistant. The field of study is a local community; perhaps just a hundred or so individuals, seldom many more than 2000. Initially the principal researchers must be strangers to the community; hopefully, before they depart, they will be just the reverse. They will themselves have become members of the community, at least by adoption. They will have come to understand the socio-cultural system from the inside through direct participation in the network of transactions which constitutes the daily life of those who are being studied.

To achieve this transformation from the status of unwelcome stranger to that of fictive kinsman calls for great tact and patience. A high level of linguistic competence is obviously an advantage but a flair for friendship is more important than an impeccable accent or a perfect lexicon.

But what is this paragon of a social anthropologist trying to find out? It is important here to distinguish between the short-term objectives of the fieldworker and the longer-term objectives of the anthropological theorist. Many of the best known theorists in social and cultural anthropology have themselves done very little practical field research and their writings often give a quite false impression of the normal tribulations of anthropological practice. This practice seems to be very much the same no matter whether the personal orientation of the research worker is materialist or idealist, Marxist or anti-Marxist, structuralist or functionalist, rationalist or empiricist.

Different practitioners would justify these common activities in many different ways. My own version goes something like this: (a) I am trying to comprehend a totality which might be called the 'way of life' of the people under study; (b) this 'way of life' consists of the acting out of an endlessly repeated social drama. The characters in the drama, the social roles, are more or less fixed, as are their mutual relationships which constitute the dramatic plot. But the way the roles are played varies from occasion to occasion according to which particular individual is playing which particular part at any particular time.

This distinction between the roles in a drama and the actors who play the roles corresponds to the fact that the data of field research must always be looked at in two dimensions. The observer must distinguish between what people actually do and what people say that they do; that is between normal custom as individually interpreted on the one hand and normative rules on the other.

When they come to write up the results of their research different anthropologists will, for doctrinal reasons, give very different weight to these two major aspects of the data, but, in the field, the anthropologist must always pay attention to both sides. He must not only distinguish behaviour from ideology, he must also take careful note of just how they are interrelated.

In so far as my own kind of social anthropology can be

considered 'structuralist' as well as 'functionalist', it is because I feel that the structuralism of Lévi-Strauss, which pays close attention to the semantic patterning of concepts which operate as normative ideas, has given us new insights into this traditional problem.

Anthropological textbooks, along with the arrangement of the university syllabus, usually give the impression that an alien way of life can always be analysed according to a more or less standard set of chapter headings which divide up the total field into sub-sections denoted by the English language words: economics, kinship, politics, law, religion, magic, myth, ritual. This is misleading for two quite separate reasons. First, most professional anthropologists use these words as if they were technical terms, but there is no general agreement about how this should be done. Secondly, this list of headings conveys a quite false impression of how field research is conducted. No experienced fieldworking anthropologist in his senses would try to subdivide his observations into categories of this sort.

It is true that there is always an all-pervasive 'economic' dimension which enters into every aspect of social life. The ethnographic data which Marxist anthropologists discuss under the headings 'modes of production' and 'relations of production' are of central importance in any kind of holistic, functionalist analysis. Every fieldworker needs to acquire some insight into the basic infrastructure of the society he is studying.

In part this means seeing who teams up with whom in what kind of work situation and why, but it also means looking at the facts in quantitative terms. It means making maps, and counting heads, and measuring fields and crop yields, and taking account of such ecological factors as climate and soil and protein resources and whatever. But, since there is really no limit to what it might be desirable to know about such matters, the sensible fieldworking anthropologist will recognize his limitations of resources, time and expertise. Social anthropology is not just a branch of biochemistry. Even the most comprehensive understanding of the ecology and of the prevailing modes of production will tell us very little that is sociologically interesting about the human society that is under observation.

But my other notional chapter headings are not of this same very general, limitless sort; nor are they all on a par. As now used in ordinary English three of these key words have a quite specific institutional reference while the others are extremely vague. *Politics* describes a specialized field of activity concerned with the whole machinery of government; *law* correspondingly refers to the whole apparatus of the machinery of justice; *religion* to that which concerns the activities of churches and churchmen. The division of labour in modern Britain is such that these three major segments of social life can be thought of as distinct and virtually autonomous sub-systems, each with its own set of specialized self-perpetuating roles – ministers, 'politicians', civil servants, judges, lawyers, policemen, bishops, clergy – all of which are open, at least in theory, to any individual of appropriate age, sex, and education who chooses to make himself a candidate.

By contrast, the terms kinship, magic, myth and ritual, are devoid of any general agreed meaning and are not tied in with any clearly identifiable set of representative social roles. Yet anthropologists regularly write as if this whole rag-bag of English language categories together form a unified matrix from which the sub-divisions of a scholarly discourse can be developed. The paradoxes which then result are very numerous.

Can societies which lack either law courts or judges be said to have a system of law? It clearly distorts the English concept of law if one says that they have, but there are scores of anthropological monographs which claim to be concerned with systems of 'primitive' law.

Likewise, if anthropologists used the word *religion* in the sense in which it is ordinarily used by ordinary speakers of English, where it is tied in with such compartmentalized matters as church membership and a professional priesthood, then it would have no application at all to most of the societies which anthropologists usually study. Yet anthropologists regularly write monographs about particular 'primitive' religions and even about 'primitive religion' in general.

Such books are in fact mainly concerned with systems of cosmological belief. There might be some advantage if anthropologists regularly wrote about 'cosmology' rather than about 'religion', if only because the former word is not much used by ordinary speakers of ordinary English.

As for *magic*, which readers of Frazer's *The Golden Bough* might suppose to lie at the very centre of the anthropologist's interests, I can only say that, after a lifetime's career as a professional anthropologist, I have almost reached the conclusion that the word has no meaning whatever.

And so also with 'myth' and 'ritual'. I write about these themes myself but often only for want of a better language. What I mean by these categories differs quite substantially from what other well-known anthropologists mean. Confusion is inevitable. I would like to get rid of both terms but I am not sure how to do it. But I would retain 'politics'.

In the past the term 'politics' has caused great confusion when applied to non-European societies. The ethnography of the colonial era was grossly distorted by the widely held assumption (shared by administrators and anthropologists alike) that all forms of political leadership can be satisfactorily subsumed under a single role stereotype: 'the native chief'. On the other hand one of the standard definitions of the term 'politics' is 'the art of rallying support to a cause in which you are interested'[2] and that is part of the fabric of social life in any sort of social system. Anyway, whatever label he chooses to use, the organization of leadership and of the power that goes with it, is certainly one of the matters to which the field anthropologist needs to pay close attention.

'Kinship' poses a different kind of problem. The study of 'kinship' really does lie at the very heart of social anthropology and anthropologists argue a great deal among themselves about just what the word is supposed to mean. What they tend to overlook is that the very idea that kinship can be thought of as a dimension of the total society, analogous to, yet quite distinct from, both 'economics' and 'politics', is an invention of the anthropologists themselves.

Kinship in social anthropology

This last point needs elaboration. Novice readers of anthropological monographs should not suppose that the technical sense in which the term 'kinship' is being employed bears any close relationship to the kinship with which they are already familiar as the result of their own domestic experience.

Novice anthropologists are not all birds of a feather but most readers of this book are likely to have grown up in a modern industrialized society of the sort which presupposes a particular type of major distinction between private affairs and public affairs. One good reason why such people (if they want to become anthropologists) should start off by studying a cultural system which is radically different from their own is that they can thereby undergo the traumatic experience of discovering that, in other societies, this deeply emotive private/public distinction may operate in quite a different way.

With us privacy and kinship are felt to be roughly coterminous. Kin are those with whom we adopt the special style of informal communication which is adopted towards members of the immediate domestic family who are treated in this specially favoured way even when they do not live all together in one household.

The narrowest such 'we'-group is that of the domestic family itself, parents and their young children and their co-resident retainers (if there are any), but the category 'kinsmen' also embraces grandparents and grandchildren, married siblings and their children, married children, uncles and aunts, first cousins, and perhaps a few more. Such people are all privileged in limited degree even when they reside elsewhere. We treat them quite differently from strangers or even from neighbours. Kinsmen, in this sense, are related to me in a special private way. But the number of individuals whom I will treat in this intimate fashion is quite small; perhaps a score, seldom much more.

In most human societies the social field is cut up in other ways. The 'we'-group solidarity which we associate with the intimacy of kinship, in the sense just described, tends to ramify outwards through the whole social system. The opposition kinsman/neighbour scarcely exists because all neighbours are likely to be reckoned as kin of one sort or another.

This need not mean that the private/public distinction vanishes altogether but it applies to different domains. For example, with us, homicide is the prototype public offence, it is a *crime* which automatically results in the intervention of the police, whereas most breaches of sexual morality are matters of concern only to members of the domestic household and their close kin. But in many societies the position is exactly reversed; homicide invites private reprisal, while many types of sexual offence lead to public punishment because they are regarded as *sins* which generate a condition of ritual pollution and thus endanger the whole community.

It is empirical facts of this general kind which justify the fieldworking anthropologist in putting domestic relationships at the very centre of his research interests.

But here I must draw a distinction of rather a different kind, namely that between biological relationship and social relationship. Of course we are all very well aware that the distinction exists and that a man's *genitor*, who made his mother pregnant, was not necessarily the same individual as his *pater*, the legally recognized father, the husband of his mother. But because, in terms of our Christian moral code, this is a shameful matter we are inclined to push it to one side and to assume that kinship is the equivalent of 'blood relationship' which implies, or should imply, biological connection.

In social anthropology this becomes important for a variety of reasons. One of these was mentioned earlier on. Geneticists and sociobiologists are only interested in kinship of the biological sort so when they dip into monographs written by social anthropologists they are predisposed to imagine that the anthropologists' references to 'kinship' are to biological kinship. As a rule this is not the case and grave confusions can result.

But of greater importance for the social anthropologists themselves is that in many societies the distinction between biological kinship and sociological kinship is quite clearly recognized and the degree of their identification or dissociation is a matter of formal rules: 'Copulation and marriage are *not* the same thing' or: 'Copulation and marriage *are* the same thing' as the case may be.

And finally there is the difference of range. The range over which we can be sure, or think we can be sure, of biological connection is always very narrow; but sociological kinship, which depends only on our willingness to slot individuals into particular verbal categories, can be extended as far as we like, or rather as far as local convention requires, and that may be thousands of miles and include many thousands of individuals.

Here I must emphasize that, although social anthropologists in the field concentrate a great deal of their attention on day-to-day domestic relationships, it is not really the set of domestic relationships as such which is their ultimate focus of interest. It is rather that social anthropologists have learnt from experience that the totality of the local community is usually treated by its members as an expanded domestic household; though equally well one might say that a domestic household is treated as a fined down version of the total community. In either case, the anthropologist, in studying the domestic group and its interconnections with other domestic groups, finds that he is also studying, in model form, the structure of the local community and its interconnections with other local communities.

In such circumstances the language of kinship – that is to say the set of words which fulfil the domestic purposes of the English words 'father', 'mother', 'brother', 'sister', 'uncle', 'aunt', and so on – is used to denote what we might otherwise be inclined to regard as economic, political, legal or religious relationships. But words which serve such comprehensive purposes are clearly very different kinds of words from the ordinary English terms 'father', 'mother' etc., which have a much more restricted scope.

This particular linguistic pitfall has in the past led to a vast amount of anthropological confusion; it still does. When you read anything that any anthropologist has written on the topic of kinship terminology be on your guard. The argument may not mean what you think; the author himself may not have understood what he is saying.

With that warning let me briefly say something about the general topic. The comparative study of kinship terminologies is one of the longest established traditions in academic anthropology. It goes back to work published by Morgan in 1871 and still has its committed devotees, especially in France and the United States.

The basis of the whole exercise is the assumption that, in any ordinary human language, the set of terms which can be glossed as 'father', 'mother', 'brother', 'sister' etc., because of the way that they are employed within the context of the domestic family, is somehow primary and basic. The morpheme which is glossed as 'father' may have extended meanings when it is used in other contexts, but its *real* meaning is 'father' in its ordinary English sense of 'male parent'.

The total set of such terms (that is to say the words in themselves without reference to any associated set of behaviours) is said to constitute 'the kinship system' of the society concerned. It is then claimed that a great variety of fundamental facts concerning the structure and social organization of the society can be directly inferred from a close analysis of 'the kinship system' in this verbal sense.

The literature relating to this branch of anthropology is immense; some of it is very sophisticated in form, even mathematical. Many of the matters which are discussed within this framework are of the greatest importance for social anthropology. Nevertheless, from my point of view, by far the greater part of this material is completely misleading because it fails to take account of the fact that while kinship words in most European languages are applied, with rare exceptions, only to relationships within the private domain and thus have quite specific meanings, the corresponding words in most other languages are highly polysemic.

There are no grounds whatever for insisting that the private/domestic meaning of such words is primary and the public/community-wide meanings secondary.

Here once again we see the advantage that comes to the novice anthropologist who learns his craft as a stranger within a speech community which is totally alien. Learning the meaning of verbal categories from scratch is difficult and time-consuming but it is very instructive. The anthropologist who goes about things in this hard way ought not to fall into the error of supposing that kinship is 'a thing in itself'.

The language of kinship and the behaviours which the use of such language provokes are social devices for giving expression to networks of relationship. But the relationships thus expressed are multifaceted; they stretch outward through the whole society, they are not simply domestic. Where social anthropologists write about 'kinship', other kinds of scholar might discuss 'property' (the relationship between individuals and things or between individuals and land), or 'politics' (the power-loaded relationship between individuals and other individuals).

Once that is understood then the answer to my original question: What is it that social anthropologists actually do? becomes easier to understand. For the answer is that they spend a very great deal of their time observing how and when and where kinship relationships are brought into play, and in trying to understand the discriminations which mark the boundary between kinship relationships and non-kinship relationships. And here, once again, we are in an area where the inherent ambiguity of the continuity/discontinuity opposition becomes very noticeable.

Much of the difficulty stems from the ethos of individualism which is central to the contemporary Western society but which is notably absent from most of the societies which social anthropologists study. We expect, or say that we expect, that individuals will be appointed to social offices of all kinds in their individual capacity and on the basis of their individual merit. This does not in fact happen, but in other kinds of social system people do not even pretend that it happens.

Typically, the anthropologist finds that individuals hold titular offices by virtue of their position in the kinship system. Offices are deemed to be permanently related to one another in a structure of kinship. This is a simple enough idea but when the same structure is made to apply to government, labour relations, the administration of justice, or mystical communication according to context, we find it confusing.

A good example of such kinship-based overlap of social roles can be found in the various volumes of Malinowski's classic, though incomplete, account of the Trobriand community of Omarakana. We there meet with various semi-stylized characters described as 'the Paramount Chief', 'the Canoe Owner' (*toliwaga*), 'the Village Headman', 'the Garden Magician' and so on. The story as a whole only begins to make sense when the reader appreciates that, in appropriate circumstances, all these roles might be filled by one and the same individual. But he would do so by virtue of his position in the kinship network not because of his personal qualities.

The model attributes of a 'primitive' society

As I have indicated in several other places in this book, the distinction which is frequently drawn between 'primitive' societies, which have 'elementary' structures and which exist outside history, and 'advanced' societies, which have 'complex' structures and are consciously involved in the processes of historical transformation, is much less clear-cut than has often been suggested.

It is true that literacy seems to generate a sense of rigidly structured social order and a consciousness of historical change which is qualitatively different from the loose structural metaphors and the 'mythological' view of the past which anthropologists usually encounter in 'wild' (*sauvage*) societies. Yet what Eliade has called 'the myth of the eternal return' is just as characteristic of Hinduism, with its elaborate literary traditions, as it is of the totemism of the Australian Aborigines. In my own view there is no significant discontinuity in terms of either structure or form between 'modern' societies and 'primitive' societies. The social anthropologist can find what he is looking for in either.

All the same, simply in terms of precedent, it seems clear that social anthropologists usually study 'primitive' societies. There is no particular reason why they should, but that is what they mostly like to do.

But, in those terms, taking the very wide range of social systems which were studied by the first generation of British social anthropologists as a model (the list includes the Trobrianders, the Tikopia, the Bemba, the Tswana, the Azande, the Nuer, the Nupe, and the Tallensi among others), is it possible to formulate a useful stereotype of what this notional entity 'a primitive society' or 'a savage (wild) society' is like?

The answer is: No! However there are plenty of useless stereotypes around and since they influence the way anthropologists write up their monographs I ought to say something about them.

The following are some of the features that have been said to be characteristic of primitive societies.

1. *They are homogeneous.*

In the course of his fieldwork the anthropologist will observe in considerable detail the day-to-day interactions of a few hundred individuals with many of whom he will eventually become intimately acquainted. If he then writes a monograph about a 'tribe' or a 'people' or a 'social system' and he wants to be recognized as a scientist rather than as an artist, he is under pressure to persuade himself (and his readers) that the events which he saw happening before his eyes were 'typical' of what might be going on elsewhere in the system. Homogeneity is then introduced as an axiom; it cannot be demonstrated.

This part of the model is highly suspect. In the past, anthropologists have made the most exaggerated claims concerning the supposed typicality of their observations. Latterly it has become increasingly apparent that neighbouring small-scale communities, even when they are lumped together under the same 'tribal' label, are just as likely to be sharply contrasted as they are to be very much the same. The contrast may itself be a significant feature of the overall pattern. The question whether what the social anthropologist describes is or is not typical of anything in a statistical sense seems to me totally irrelevant.

2. *They are segmented.*

The population under study is not dispersed at random across the map but consists of individuals who conceive of themselves as belonging to enduring groups which have continuity in a time scale measured in generations rather than in years.

Such groups may cohere together according to a wide variety of principles, e.g. by identification with a particular locality, a particular herd of livestock, a particular parcel of seed (annually replaced), a particular lineage name transmitted from parent to child, and so on. Since recruitment is mainly by procreation it necessarily follows that, in most cases, a substantial proportion of any such population will be related to one another as biological kin; but just how they are related cannot be known and, from a social anthropological point of view, this fact of biological kinship is of no great interest. The crucial point is that, in most cases, group identity is expressed by the people concerned in the language of kinship. Whatever else 'we' may be, 'we' are kinsmen.

Alternatively, where the members of the single community under study perceive themselves as belonging to a number of separate kin groups which do not intermarry, this is a matter of great sociological significance regardless of what may or may not be the actual biological facts of the case.

The same principle also applies on a larger scale. As we move across the map the members of a particular community, 'A', will perceive their relationship to the members of another community, 'B', to be either that of kinsmen or of non-kinsmen and the distinction is likely to be of critical 'political' importance.

In many human societies virtually everyone is treated as a kinsman of one sort or another so that alliances established by marriage are simply the renewal of links which have also existed in the past. Lévi-Strauss' arguments about the 'elementary structures of kinship' only apply to societies of this kind. But there is also a wide variety of technologically quite unsophisticated social systems in which social stratification, political subordination and class exploitation are linked to the kinsman/non-kinsman distinction. For example, it is often the case that the essential characteristic of a 'slave' is not that he is in a servile position or economically disadvantaged but that, not being a kinsman, he is denied the rights of a full human being.

In such cases the act of converting a non-kinsman into a kinsman (e.g., through marriage or adoption) can have major political implications. In a great many social systems the only fully legitimate marriages are those in which the bride and bridegroom are not only already kin but kin of a specific category such as, say, that which includes the relationship mother's brother's daughter/father's sister's son. The rules are formally protected by supposedly powerful religious taboos, breach of which will result in supernatural punishment for all concerned. Yet we often find that in such societies the arrangement of highly unorthodox marriage alliances between 'wrongly related' kinsmen or between non-kinsmen is an essential part of the fabric of small-scale politics through which men of influence build up their power. Once again the normal and the normative must be distinguished.

All this simply reinforces my earlier point that not only must the field anthropologist pay close attention to the difference between normative rules and social practice but that the study of kinship is something far more complicated than simply the study of genealogies or the ramifying biological links of the domestic family.

3. *They are mythopoeic.*
The state of how things are, as evidenced by who has rights over what and over whom, is justified by 'myth', that is to say by tales about the past which have a sacred or religious quality (after the fashion of the Christian Bible), rather than by legislative enactments or precedents recorded in historical documents.

Furthermore this mythological-cosmological justification of the ordering of the prevailing social system is recurrently exhibited in 'rituals' of various kinds. These may include sacrifices, shamanistic trances, divinations, magical performance, sorcery, and even the curing of the sick. This last because illness tends to be attributed to supernatural causes so that the art of healing is, from another aspect, part of the more general art of communicating with supernatural powers.

It is this range of performances rather than any coherent body of theology which most social anthropologists have in mind when they refer to the magico-religious system. But since the actors concerned are ordinary members of the community, who probably conceive of themselves not only as kinsmen to one another but also as kinsmen of the supernatural beings whose mythology is being enacted, it once again becomes crucial that the investigator should fully understand the nuances of the kinship language in which the multifaceted relationships between the living and the dead are being expressed.

I am not suggesting that you take this model too seriously. If 'primitive societies' are what social anthropologists study then some primitive societies fit the model quite well. Others do not. But the model does provide an explanation of why fieldworking anthropologists set about things in the way they do.

The first essential of intensive fieldwork is that the fieldworker should be able to recognize everyone in his vicinity, not just as a set of individuals but as a set of individuals holding named titles to office who consider themselves to be related to one another in a particular way.

The second essential is that he should be able to gain most of his information by direct observation of how these people organize their day-to-day affairs both in space and time. How do they arrange the patterning of their domestic environment, their settlements, their houses, their productive and reproductive activities? How do they behave towards one another in the great diversity of situations which may arise within this patterned context? Such observations have value because, although the situations may be diverse, the patterning tends to recur and the web of kinship which links the individuals together persists all the way through. In this way the fieldworker will come to see that this mesh of kinship behaviour is a manifestation of the social structure, a visible expression of who controls what.

But the researcher must use his ears as well as his eyes. 'Social structure' belongs to the metaphysics of anthropology. Part of the fieldworker's problem is to discover how this abstract schema is expressed in the verbal statements by which his informants describe their cosmology.

Just how complicated a problem this may turn out to be is indicated by the following quotations from the opening paragraphs of the first two chapters of Christine Hugh-Jones' very remarkable book *From the Milk River*, which is a study of Pira-pirana Indians living in the Vaupes region of Colombia, as viewed from the perspective of the inhabitants of a single longhouse community in which she and her husband resided for two years between September 1968 and December 1970:

Pira-pirana Indians see themselves as existing within an ordered cosmos created in the ancestral past. The world of their present-day experience is a residue or product of the ancestral doings related in myth, ritual chants, and shamanic spells. From their own point of view, this cosmos and the mythical deeds associated with it control their contemporary social life and provide a moral framework for present-day action . . . I work the other way round . . . I start with the building of basic units of social structure, families and patrilineal groups, through marriage and procreation. I begin by showing how different phases of that temporal process are associated with different spaces in and around the longhouse and end by showing that the very same 'space-time' principles underlie the structure of the cosmos . . . The anthropologist must regard the ancestral cosmos as an imaginary projection of present experience, but at the same time it is a projection which both controls present experience and forms an integral part of it. There is therefore a sense in which each world – the ancestral world and the present-day secular one – regulates the other . . . The anthropologist's social structure must be pieced together from a muddling mass of statements that Indians make about kinship connections, group names, ancestral derivations, linguistic affiliations, geographical sites, and so on . . . [3]

There is no golden rule about how this 'muddling mass' should be sorted out apart from the absolute necessity for patience and sympathy. In the fieldwork situation the anthropologist's aim must be that his informants should treat him as their pupil and that they should be prepared to teach him their way of life by accepting him as a kinsman, so that, as near as may be, he becomes 'one of us'.

This kind of rapport is difficult to achieve and it entails an entirely different relationship between the informant and his pupil from that which was assumed by the anthropologists of seventy years ago. In those days the fieldworker retained his status as a privileged stranger and proceeded to make a catalogue of ancient manners and customs much as if he were a policeman investigating a crime. I have the impression that there are still quite a number of anthropological research workers who conduct their enquiries by such question and answer methods, but they are gradually being superseded. Custom that has been experienced as part of daily life is not at all the same thing as custom that is described in a formal interview.

In a book such as this I cannot say more than that about how the modern fieldworking anthropologist conducts his research. In fieldwork it is the details that matter and details cannot be discussed in general terms. If you really want to understand what anthropologists do you will have to do it yourself. The next best thing is to read, with real care and attention, detailed accounts of modern fieldwork such as are provided by the two Hugh-Jones volumes. Concentrate on the details of a single system; do not expect to arrive at generalizations by picking up ethnographic snippets from here, there and everywhere. But don't delude yourself into thinking that either the practice of fieldwork or the understanding of other people's fieldwork is at all easy. The totality of the way of life of even the simplest sort of human society is exceedingly complex.

5 Debt, Relationship, Power

Throughout my last chapter I kept on emphasizing that the task of the social anthropologist in the field is not simply to observe the details of customary behaviour but to note how this behaviour serves to 'express relationships'.

In terms of anthropological theory, this chapter, taken as a whole, may be considered an elaboration of Radcliffe-Brown's formula that the core of social anthropology is the study of society considered as 'a structure of person to person relationships'. I suspect however that parts of my treatment of this theme would have been very uncongenial to Radcliffe-Brown himself. Other parts of my argument derive from Malinowski, Mauss and Lévi-Strauss, as well as from various of my younger contemporaries. I shall not attempt to distinguish the particular sources of individual ideas.

In the language of social anthropology *person* is sharply distinguished from *individual*. The individual is a living biological animal who is born, develops to maturity, grows old and dies; the person is the set of offices and roles which attach to the individual at any particular stage in his life career.

Parts of an individual's day-to-day behaviour are quite idiosyncratic; in general, these fall outside the scope of social anthropology. But very often the major part of an individual's activities stem from the duties and reciprocal obligations which fall to him by virtue of his roles as a social person. The *network of person-to-person relationships* formula thus refers to sets of rights and duties which find expression in more or less predictable patterns of behaviour. When ethnographers refer to *customs*, the behaviours in question are always of this semi-obligatory predictable kind.

All person-to-person relationships entail reciprocity. Individual 'A', by virtue of his position in society, has rights and duties *vis-à-vis* individual 'B'. But individual 'B' in turn, by virtue of *his* position, has complementary rights and duties *vis-à-vis* individual 'A'. The reciprocal/ complementary behaviours of the two individuals 'A' and 'B', in their interactions with one another, may be said to *symbolize* or *express* the relationship between them. But I must emphasize that this concept of *relationship* is an abstraction, an invention of the observing anthropologist. As far as the actors themselves are concerned their mutual relationship *is* their mutual interactive behaviour.

Interactive behaviour, in this sense, can take many forms. Small infants smile at their mothers who smile back; the infant cries, the mother puts the infant to her breast. In mature persons interaction is usually initiated by speech; but in ordinary life, *isolated* speech interaction, as in a telephone conversation, is rare. The more normal situation is for every exchange of words to take place in a context which allows the verbal activity to be associated with other kinds of activity and other kinds of message.

Thus the English greet one another with a verbal formula, a reciprocal, 'How do you do?', but simultaneously they shake hands. Neighbours affirm their friendship by recip- rocal hospitality. More distant friends exchange letters or Christmas cards, and so on. In all these cases the reciprocity is *like-for-like* and the message that is encoded in the action is roughly: 'We are friends and we are of equal status.'

But the majority of person-to-person exchanges are not of

this like-for-like kind. Correspondingly most of the persons in a close network of relationships are of unequal rather than equal status. The inequality of the exchange is congruent with the inequality of the status.

For example, in most work situations in our capitalist world the employer gives money in exchange for the employee's labour. In the dyad *employer/employee* the relationship is specified and recognizable in terms of who gives what to whom. And so it is right across the board. Social person labels, such as *teacher, pupil, doctor, patient, master, servant*, only acquire meaning when they are brought into association with their dyadic counterpart as in *teacher/pupil, doctor/patient, master/servant*. We can then recognize what the relationship is by observing, in context, who gives what to whom.

Failure to see the general principle that lies behind such simple, common-knowledge, facts as these has often led anthropologists to write a great deal of nonsense. This applies especially to the area in which anthropologists consider themselves especially expert – the field of kinship relationships.

Thus it should be obvious (but apparently is not!) that a single kinship category word such as *father* can never denote an isolated individual. It is only one half of several, separable, dyadic relationships, notably: *father/foetus, father/infant child, father/son, father/daughter*. In relational terms the behaviours involved in these four cases may be very different even within a single social context.

But I have already warned you to be on your guard against anything that any anthropologist has ever written about kinship terminologies, so I will not pursue the matter here. But the basic trouble with this literature is implicit in my example. The authors concerned assume that the word 'father' (or its equivalent in other languages) has a single meaning in itself, whereas in fact it has many different meanings depending upon what other term forms the other half of the dyadic relationship.

But to get back to exchange. Although behavioural reciprocity is implicit in the very idea of relationship, the reciprocity is, as a general rule, neither immediate nor complete.

So far I have given the impression that, if we use the notion of *gift* in the widest possible sense, then gift exchanges constitute the visible expression of what social anthropologists clumsily describe as networks of person-to-person relationships. But that account of my overall argument needs to be qualified in one very major respect.

The structure of the relational network is only accessible to the outside observer to the extent that it is visibly manifested in gift-giving performance, but, for the insiders, the actors who actually operate the system, this same structure is felt to consist of rights and obligations. It is not so much a network of gift-giving as a network of indebtedness.

This has very important implications for our interpretation of the coded significance of gift-exchange behaviour. From the actor's point of view, the great majority of gift-giving transactions are partial repayments of debt. I would emphasize the word *partial*. In any context, if a debt is ever fully paid off then the relationship between debtor and creditor ceases to exist.

Now some relationships are of just this kind. If I go to the market to buy a dozen eggs I pay the full price there and then. I have no residual obligation to come back to the same market stall next week. However, if I am a regular customer and the stall owner gives me credit because I happen to be short of cash, I do have an obligation to come back. And when I return I shall no doubt make another purchase and so on. Indeed that is what the label *regular customer* really means: *a customer who has the potential to go into debt.* And all *enduring* relationships have this quality; when the relationship is activated the parties concerned engage in gift exchange, but at all other times, while the relationship is quiescent, it exists only as a feeling of indebtedness – that is of rights and obligations between the parties.

Within this very general framework a number of variations may occur though the range of possibilities is not really very great. Let us consider some of them.

1. The simplest exchanges are unpremeditated and tit-for-tat: children engaged in aggressive play; adults exchanging drinks around a pub bar in token of temporary trust and friendship; casual conversation with a stranger on a bus. The reciprocity usually takes the form of direct equivalence: an eye for an eye, a glass of beer for a glass of beer.

Narrowly dyadic relationships of this kind show no tendency to proliferate outwards so as to form a wider network, and, since they are usually short-lived, anthropologists have not often given them much attention. But some forms of enduring relationships have also been said to have this form. Lévi-Strauss rates sister-exchange marriage as belonging to his category *restricted exchange*, by which he means 'non-proliferating', but my next variation really fits his typology rather better.

2. As we have seen, whenever the payment of the return gift is postponed, the relationship between creditor and debtor is extended in time. But this will only be the case if the debt continues to be remembered as an unrequited obligation by both parties to the transaction. In domestic relationships within the household and in relationships between close neighbours, who see one another very frequently, this is how gift exchange usually operates. There

is no close accounting of who owes what to whom but there is a tacit understanding by all concerned that there is a moral obligation to balance things out over a period.

In many of the simpler agricultural societies this is also the normal way to organize labour; no wages are paid, but, over a period, each household pays back in labour form whatever it has previously received in labour form. Wherever I have observed transactions of this kind the balancing of accounts has been very carefully worked out.

Most of the customary marriage arrangements which Lévi-Strauss rates as *restricted exchange* have this delayed reciprocity aspect. The *alliance* between the groups which exchange women under a sister-exchange marriage rule or under a rule which specifies marriage between a man and his father's sister's daughter persists through time because of the felt obligation to arrange, at a future date, the counterpart of a marriage which has already taken place.

The underlying general principle has already been stated: persisting relationships only exist as feelings of indebtedness. From time to time every such persisting debt relationship needs to be made manifest in an actual gift transaction, but the relationship is in the feeling of indebtedness not in the gift.

3. My third variation corresponds to what Lévi-Strauss calls *generalized exchange*. The reciprocity is asymmetrical and in consequence it has a proclivity for extending outwards into a network. Most of the trading arrangements which are encountered in modern industrial societies follow this pattern. If I wish to buy a manufactured object from a shopkeeper, the shopkeeper must first obtain it from a wholesaler, the wholesaler must then in turn obtain it from the manufacturer, who must in turn obtain components and raw materials from other suppliers further down the line. There will be no point in the proceedings at which the gifts

which have moved in one direction are directly returned in the reverse direction.

In this particular case, the reciprocal gift is usually money, but here too the transactions are open ended. In initiating my original purchase I incur an obligation to make a payment in money, but I in turn have to have a source from which I can acquire the money in the first place, and this will, directly or indirectly, put me into at least a temporary relationship with a great variety of people, including the reader who purchased this book from a bookstall and paid out money, some small fraction of which will eventually find its way back to myself.

Lévi-Strauss himself uses the notion of *generalized exchange* in a less general way. His prototype example of such a system is one in which formal custom requires a man to marry a woman of the category mother's brother's daughter. The effect of such a rule is that the lineage of the bride and the lineage of the husband are placed in an asymmetrical *wife-giver/wife-receiver* relationship; the wife-givers then receive 'valuables' of some sort in return for the women that they give away. However, since the rules of exogamy prevent the wife-givers from marrying women of their own group, they must find wives from elsewhere. The outcome, according to Lévi-Strauss, is a generalized circularity analogous to that which I described for the relationship in our commercial system between an author and his book-buying reader.

This is a highly abstract argument and there is a wide discrepancy between Lévi-Strauss' theorizing on the subject and how such 'systems of circulating connubium' actually operate. But certain parts of Lévi-Strauss' schema have application to a wide variety of ethnographic materials. For example, the famous Kula system of ritual exchange, first described by Malinowski in 1922, fits the pattern quite well.

The partners to a Kula exchange relationship are commonly members of quite different social groups; often they live in different islands and speak different languages. The relationship is of long duration and is asymmetrical. If partner 'A' has an obligation to give partner 'B' armshells (*mwali*) then partner 'B' must give back necklaces (*soulava*, *bagi*) and, vice versa, 'A' can never give back necklaces to 'B', nor can 'B' ever give armshells to 'A'.

Later research seems to show that Malinowski mis-understood a number of key features of the system he described, but it is certainly the case that the participants in the Kula conceive of it as a *circulating* system of exchange. Furthermore the overall effect of this circulation is to link together into a widely ramifying network of relationships a great number of individuals of quite different status and quite different cultural background. It is also very clear, both from Malinowski's evidence and from later research, that Kula partnerships are viewed by the participants as structures of permanent indebtedness. Any particular sequence of actual exchanges of Kula valuables serves to manifest this state of indebtedness but at the end of the day the position is as it began. The reciprocal gift-giving between the partners has in no way reduced the obligation to engage in further gift exchanges in the future.

And that brings me back to my original point. Relation-ships within society consist of the recognition that indi-viduals in their particular social roles have rights and duties *vis-à-vis* other individuals in other social roles.

But now I want to shift the argument somewhat. Structures of social relationship are not only structures of indebtedness, they are also structures of *power*. But what is *power*?

In another context, when discussing the logic of ritual symbols, I have said that 'power lies at the interface of categories'. This may sound complicated but the argument is very similar to that which Victor Turner employs when he comments on the liminality, or 'betwixt and between' status, of persons who are engaged in any ritual process.[1] My usage however is more general than Turner's and depends on a mechanical model.

As a social anthropologist I am mainly concerned with power as an aspect of the relationship between two social persons in a hierarchy: If 'A' exerts power over 'B', then the status of 'A' is superordinate and that of 'B' subordinate. We recognize the existence of such power by observing that if 'A' gives orders, 'B' obeys them.

But in English the concept of power has a physical as well as a metaphysical connotation; thus we talk of 'water power', 'steam power', 'electrical power' and so on.

In the language of engineers, power is said to 'flow' whenever the 'potential' at the two ends of a channel is unequal. For example, if the positive and negative poles of an electrical battery are connected, we ordinarily describe the discharge that is then manifested (as heat, or motive force or whatever) as a flow of power from the positive pole to the negative pole. The metal connector between the two poles then falls into my specification of 'the interface between two categories'. This interface position is one of danger. If the metal is too thin to accept the load (as with a piece of fuse wire) it will burn up.

The point of this analogy is that, so long as the two poles are separated, there is no relationship between them; no power flows; there is no danger. But as soon as the two poles are put into relationship by a 'power conductor' the relative potential at the two ends of the connector generates a power flow. The greater the difference in potential the greater the flow of power and the greater the danger to the interface/power-conductor.

And so it is also with human affairs. If a 'person-to-person relationship' is made to carry too great a 'flow of power' from the dominant to the subordinate position the connection between the two parties is likely to break up in violence.

And much the same is true of the ideological relationships which link human beings to metaphysical powers. The betwixt and between area of liminality which Turner discusses, in which social differences between individuals tend to be forgotten in a shared feeling of *communitas*, as among the participants in a pilgrimage, is the interface between human beings and 'spiritual beings'. It is a position of danger where miracles of healing may occur but miracles of disaster also.

Cynics of course would hold that the power potential and the danger that exists at the interface of the physical and the metaphysical exists only in the human imagination. But for the social anthropologist that point is hardly relevant. It is because such interfaces are *believed* to be dangerous that men act as they do in ritual situations. And for the anthropologist that is all that matters.

Religious ideology usually presupposes that the difference in power potential between human being and 'deity' is infinitely great and totally destructive; the power differentials within an ordinary domestic context are less precarious. But even so, in almost all kinds of social relationship, there is some degree of power flow. Relationships in which the two individuals concerned are of exactly equal status are very unusual.

As you can see I have set up a set of equations which can be summarized in the following formulae:

state of indebtedness	=	social relationship
payment of debt	=	manifestation of relationship
nature of payment	=	nature of relationship
reciprocal equal payments	=	equality of status; absence of power flow either way
asymmetrical payments	=	inequality of status; power flow from 'higher' to 'lower'

Further, each statement is reversible. Every social relationship entails a state of indebtedness just as every state of indebtedness entails a social relationship.

There are several grounds for putting the argument in this way. First of all it brings out the functionalist point that the different 'aspects' of social relationship, in the fields of kinship, economy, politics, law, religion etc., are all versions of the same thing. Each mode of expressing a particular relationship is metaphoric of all the others.

Secondly it helps to show just how far this functionalist/-structuralist style of argument is, or is not, compatible with Marxist presentations. The Marxist thesis that power lies with whoever controls the 'means of production', is usually mixed up with an egalitarian thesis that each producer has a natural moral right to the power which his production generates. This does not fit squarely with my equations but it is not unrelated to them. Notice for example that the left side of each equation suggests 'economic' relationship, while the right side suggests, in the first instance, the domestic relationships of kinship and the political relationships of governmental authority.

Marx and Engels recognized this interlocking equivalence right from the start though they confused the issue by trying to fit their argument into a social evolutionist framework. The following quotation comes from Engels' Preface to the first (1884) edition of *The Origin of the Family*, which was a kind of rewrite, in precis, of Morgan's *Ancient Society* (1877):

> According to the materialist conception, the determining factor in history is, in the final instance, the production and reproduction of the immediate essentials of life. This, again, is' of a twofold character. On the one side the production of the means of existence, of articles of food and clothing, dwellings, and of the tools necessary for that production; on the other side, the production of human beings themselves, the propagation of the species.

Engels then went on to assert that:

> The social organization under which the people of a particular historical epoch and a particular country live is determined by both kinds of production, by the stage of development of labour on the one hand and of the family on the other.

Subsequent research by anthropologists has failed to confirm this latter generalization. There does not seem to be any close relationship between 'modes of production', 'relations of (economic) production', 'relations of political domination' and 'forms of the family' (i.e. relations of human reproduction). Nevertheless the anthropologist's favourite stamping ground, 'the study of kinship', becomes arid and thoroughly misleading if the anthropologist concerned ever allows himself to forget that the domestic household, which stands at the core of any kinship system when viewed from the inside, is a social machine for the production of the means of subsistence and the reproduction of human beings.

My phrase 'viewed from the inside' is crucial. The fundamental novelty about social anthropology, as it has developed since the days of Malinowski, is that the fieldworking anthropologist tries to understand alien societies from the inside rather than from the outside. He does not look at society from afar, through the wrong end of a telescope, as is the usual practice of professional historians. The anthropologist takes a worm's eye view. Through partial participation in the events and networks of relationships which he observes all around him, he tries to understand how it feels to be a member of the society in question. At best, that understanding is only partial, but anthropologists would claim that they have a much better insight into the motives and perceptions of 'other people' than do scholars who work within other conventions – whether they be those of pure science or of the humanities.

Most readers of this book are likely to have grown up in one or other of the many contemporary versions of what are often lumped together under the general label 'modern industrial societies'. At the micro-level of domestic, face-to-face, relations these 'modern' social systems are just as varied as the 'pre-industrial' societies which provide the data of conventional social anthropology. The generalizations which follow are derived from my own experience in one particular sector of British society during the era 1910 to 1980. The reader should not reject them outright if it so happens that they do not correspond to his own personal impressions.

One of the characteristics which distinguish 'modern industrial' from 'pre-industrial' society is that in the former there is a wide circulation of 'money', where 'money' means a *general* medium of exchange and a store of value which serves equally well as a reward for services rendered and as a means of purchasing commodities in the market. By contrast, in 'pre-industrial' societies there are often a variety of media of exchange which circulate in different social spheres but which are not interchangeable in any straight-forward fashion. For example, the *mwali* and *bagi* of the Trobriand Kula, which were mentioned earlier, are media of exchange which represent value, but it is not a monetary value which can be converted directly into fish or pig meat or yams.

In 'modern' systems the primary function of money is its use in economic transactions. Even so, where money changes hands, it is part of an exchange and thus an expression of the social relationship which exists between the two individuals concerned. Such relationships are specified by several distinguishable criteria.

First there is the question of who gives what to whom and how much. In general, the giver of a monetary gift ranks higher than the receiver, but, as between two receivers, the one who receives more ranks higher than the one who receives less. Members of capitalist systems tend to take such discrimination for granted but the logic of the exercise is far from obvious. The usual justification for paying the manager of a business a salary which is out of all proportion greater than that received by the men on the shop floor, who have direct contact with the product or with the machinery, is that the extra payment is for 'responsibility' but this is just another name for 'status in a power hierarchy'.

But in most industrial organizations the hierarchy of status and authority is marked, not only by the relative size of the total pay packet, but also by such distinctions as whether the actual payment is made on a daily, weekly, monthly or annual basis. Here the general principle is that those who receive the largest amount of money overall receive it at the least frequent intervals and rank highest in the hierarchy of power. Within any one system an annual stipend is superior to a monthly salary which is superior to a weekly wage which is superior to *ad hoc* payment by the hour.

You will notice that the greater the interval between wage payments, the longer the period during which the firm is in debt to its employee and, correspondingly, the greater the security of tenure of the employee. This fits with my earlier thesis about the general link between 'indebtedness' and 'relationship'.

However once one goes outside the immediate hierarchy of industrial relationships the symbolic implication of monetary payments becomes much more difficult to decipher. Many positions of great influence in British society are filled by individuals who carry out the duties of their office for no monetary reward at all. And in such situations it is usually the unpaid office holders who stand at the top of the hierarchy and who give orders to their wage-earning staff.

At the level of micro-sociology, where one is considering the organization of local small-scale communities and domestic households, this pattern is the norm rather than the exception. Voluntary work tends to carry higher prestige than paid work.

Marxists and feminists are inclined to see this familiar fact as a form of exploitation, and the current fashion is to be particularly scornful of the *honour* that is supposed to accrue to the unpaid housewife. But the issue is complex.

It is true that, to the indignation of many working women, current British tax rules assume that, in an ordinary domestic family, the husband is the head of the household by virtue of his being the breadwinner and in control of the family finances. In effect the law treats the household as a single social person whose position in the hierarchy of rights and obligations is measured by the monetary transactions of the unit as a whole. In a certain sense prestige accrues to the household which pays the most tax. But it is the husband who is responsible for paying it and who must acquire the money from outside in the first place.

But there are other situations (and there used to be many more) in which the social status of the household is measured by the give/take transactions of the wife rather than of the husband. And in such cases it is clearly more honourable to give than to receive. Servants rank below their employers. A woman who offers hospitality to guests is more honourable than one who has to take in lodgers for a fee. But here the presumption is that it is the wife rather than the husband who is the household head.

Moreover, according to the prevailing values of this system, any feminist housewife who successfully made good her claim to be paid a wage for her domestic chores would be reducing her status to that of a servant. Some women (and some anthropologists) might say that this would simply make explicit what is otherwise hidden by the fraudulent 'rituals' of society. But the real point is that, in contemporary Western society, the network of relations *within* the domestic household is built on an evaluation of exchange transactions which is, in certain respects, just the converse of that which operates in the capitalist world of wage relationships outside.

And that was the purpose of my digression from anthropology to the sociology of monetary exchange. In the kinds of society in which most of my readers were brought up the coding of behaviour presupposes a sharp division between what goes on within the household and transactions which link the household to the rest of society. In the pre-industrial societies, which provide the main field for anthropological enquiry, this kind of distinction is either non-existent or quite peripheral to the main field of the ordinary individual's day-to-day activities.

In such societies it is frequently the case that the individual treats all outsiders 'as if' they were kinsmen of some sort. I made the same point in the previous chapter but it may help if I give a concrete example.

Just what is meant by an 'outsider' in such cases is a matter for definition. The Kachins of North Burma, among whom I carried out much of my own fieldwork, were much inclined to rhetoric. A favourite opening to a speech, roughly equivalent to Shakespeare's 'Friends, Romans, Countrymen . . .' could be translated as: 'We, elder and younger brothers, affinal relatives, distant relatives, all mankind . . .'

The word I have here glossed as 'mankind' was *Jinghpaw*, which is the term by which the people known to the British as Kachins describe themselves. Kachins are of course well aware that there are other kinds of people who are not Jinghpaw in this sense, e.g. Burmese, Chinese, Indians, British anthropologists, and, in mythology, all these groups, including the Jinghpaw, are descended from a common original Adam and Eve. But outsiders of this extreme sort are not treated as fully normal human beings. On the other hand a Kachin will always take it for granted that anyone whom he is prepared to classify as a Jinghpaw is a kinsman of some sort. On one occasion I was present when, due to the exigencies of war, a Kachin from eastern Burma fetched up hundreds of miles away in a Kachin village in eastern Assam. It was only a matter of a few hours before the stranger had been slotted into the local kinship network; and the recognition of kinship was mutual.

What this all adds up to is that the coding of give/take relationships in fields quite remote from private domestic affairs is much closer to what the members of modern capitalist societies assume to be appropriate only for the restricted context of the domestic household than it is to the coding of power relationships within the wider context of the market economy which I was discussing earlier. In such systems, labour rewarded by money wages (if money wages are a possibility) rates lower than labour directly rewarded by reciprocal labour in kind or by the payment, often after considerable delay, of non-monetary gifts, or by hospitality and the gift of food.

Likewise it is only a few exceptional relationships which have the short-term characteristic of a money purchase in the market. Normal relationships, whether they focus on economics, or politics, or law, or religion, are all presumed to have the lifelong irrevocable quality which in our modern Western system applies only to national identity and family membership.

In such circumstances the use of kinship language to express all kinds of relationship, which is what anthropologists have now come to expect, clearly makes a lot of sense. But within this general pattern there is plenty of room for variation.

In our modern Western system the insider/outsider, 'we'/'they' opposition roughly corresponds to the distinction between kinship and non-kinship modes of reference. In the more elementary systems that we are now considering, kinship, of a general sort, is assumed to be all-pervading but there is again a discrimination between the insiders and the outsiders, 'we' and 'they'.

Just how the distinction is established varies from system to system but usually 'we', the insiders, are treated as 'true' kin. They are kinsmen because they are somehow of common substance, as with English *consanguinity*, kinship by common blood. Here the bond of kinship is treated as a part of the individual's biological nature; it endures throughout life; the individual has no choice. By contrast 'they', the outsiders, are treated as related to 'us' in a much more optional way. They are affines, allied to us by marriage. And entering upon a marriage calls for human decision.

Some anthropologists use this distinction as part of their own jargon. They write of kinship *and* marriage, or kinship *and* affinity, reserving the term kinship for kinship by common substance in the consanguine sense. And sometimes this fits the ethnographic facts in a quite straightforward way.

Where the 'we'-groups are exogamous, as is very often the case, the 'we'/'they' distinction corresponds exactly to the distinction 'those with whom we may not intermarry because they are of common substance with us'/'those with whom we may intermarry because they are not of common substance with us'. The notion of common substance is then usually associated with belief in descent from a common ancestor (or ancestress): from a male first father by male links only (patrilineal descent); from a female first mother through female links only (matrilineal descent).

Because of the accident that, in the early days, a high proportion of the best anthropological field research was carried out in societies which were made up of exogamous unilineal descent groups, many textbooks give the impression that unilineal descent is the normal pattern in primitive societies and hence that the distinction between kinship (of common substance) and affinity is normally clear-out and unambiguous. This is not in fact the case. A great many human societies operate with 'cognatic' systems of kinship, in which common ancestry is traced through both male and female links. There is then no obvious sense in which 'we', who claim to be of common substance, can differentiate ourselves, on the basis of descent alone, from 'they', who are not of our common substance.

In such cases the implicit definition of 'we' always includes some additional factor such as those mentioned on p.128. 'We' are those who live in this particular locality and whose ancestors have lived here since time immemorial, or 'we' are those who derive their livelihood from this particular piece of ancestral ground, or 'we' are those who raise our crops from a particular parcel of ancestral seed, annually renewed.

All such variations contain the same general idea: 'we', who are true kin, share a common substance through our shared links with the same ancestral past; but wherever descent is traced through both males and females the distinction between those who are unmarriageable because they rate as *true* kin and those who are marriageable because they do not so rate becomes very fuzzy. In Ancient Egypt, where the term for wife was the same as the term for sister, and men frequently married sisters who were full siblings, the distinction seems to have disappeared altogether.

It is for this reason that in this book I ordinarily use *kinship* in its wider sense. It encompasses affinity. But the reader should not forget that, even in those societies where kinship language is all-pervading, the bonds of kinship may be of several different kinds.

It may be helpful if at this point I pull together the underlying theme of the latter part of this chapter with the help of a schema. I have been elaborating the point, made much earlier on, that one of the really basic features of human thinking as it affects social action is the polarization of 'we' *versus* 'they'. In general what is permitted and expected with regard to our behaviour towards those who are classed as 'we' is either expressly forbidden or disapproved of with respect to those who rate as 'they', and vice versa. The moral distinction permitted/forbidden is thus context dependent.

In Western capitalist society the domestic household is not only the narrowest 'we'-group (see pp. 142–3), it is also by far the most important in the life history of the individual. Presumably this is fairly obvious. But those who attach value to studies of 'the family' on these grounds often overlook the fact that such domestic groups pass through a developmental cycle. Typically such a group starts out as a married couple; the couple acquire children; the children grow up, marry and set up nuclear households of their own; the original household declines in size and is finally wiped out by death.

As a consequence, not only is 'the family' (in this restricted sense) quite a different kind of entity at each phase of its development but, except in so far as the original householders own property which can be transmitted to their children, there is no continuity of the 'we'-group beyond the first generation. As we all know, the nuclear households of married children may continue to be linked by effective bonds of kinship both with the residual households of their parents and of their married siblings; but such continuing linkage is optional and, in practice, very variable.

I have argued that, in this modern capitalist context, the basic coding of behaviour concerns attitudes to monetary exchange and operates through the following paired oppositions:

'we' / 'they'

kin / non-kin

relationships are inherently permanent and cannot be cancelled out by a gift of money	relationships are inherently impermanent and are regularly cancelled out by a gift of money

true-kin (by 'common blood') / affinal kin (by marriage) [rules vary according to attitudes to divorce; divorce may convert a non-monetary relationship into a monetary relationship. Relations between affinal kin other than spouse often felt to be ambiguous and are marked by avoidance behaviour]

The contrasted model which I have proposed as characteristic of pre-industrial, 'elementary', societies is this:

'we' / 'they'

true-kin / affines and potential affines

'those with whom we may not intermarry' / 'those with whom we may intermarry'

relationship inherently permanent; need not be validated by gift exchange. / relationship inherently impermanent; needs to be validated by gift exchange (e.g. 'bride-price', 'dowry')

By the 'permanence' of true-kin relationships in both models I refer to the fact that if two individuals consider themselves to be true kinsmen their kinship will persist in latent form even if they do not interact with one another at all for years on end. Gift exchange will still be necessary if the rights and duties which are inherent in such relationships are to be activated, but the nature of the exchange will be quite different from that which validates the impermanent relationships in my two right-hand columns.

True kinsmen, who are in *permanent* relationship, activate their mutual status by giving one another appropriate perishable (i.e. *impermanent*) gifts, e.g. labour, food and drink, hospitality. Affinal kinsmen (in elementary societies) and non-kinsmen (in capitalist societies), who are in *impermanent* relationship, may activate their mutual status by perishable gifts of a very similar kind, but, in addition, they exchange imperishable (*permanent*) forms of gift, e.g. women, slaves, individually identifiable live animals, material valuables, and, in capitalist societies, money.

This is the essential logic of asymmetrical circulating exchange systems of the Kula type, which I mentioned earlier in the context of my discussion of *generalized* exchange and which so puzzled Malinowski. Malinowski recognized that, at least in part, the partners in Kula exchanges seemed to have utilitarian motives. They exchanged perishable consumer goods which were mutually valuable in the ordinary fashion of barter trade. But the Kula itself simply drove identifiable valuables round in a circle giving no utilitarian advantage to anyone.

In actual fact the exchange of Kula valuables does a good deal more than that, though to explain how this comes about would require an extended discussion of Melanesian ethnography which would not be appropriate. But I am making a more general point. The exchange of what Engels called 'the immediate essentials of life' – food and clothing, useful tools, women in their capacity as potential mothers – takes place between 'friends' rather than 'enemies'. True-kin do not necessarily love one another, but it is always presumed that they are friends until they are shown to be enemies. By contrast, non-kin and affines are presumed to be enemies until they are shown to be friends! In many tribal societies this fact is explicit. On quite a number of occasions ethnographers have been told by their informants that: 'we marry our enemies'.

Or, to put it the other way round, affines only remain friends so long as they remain affines; they are bonded together by political alliance rather than by common substance, and, if the parties concerned want to maintain that alliance, they must repeatedly reaffirm that bonding by the appropriate exchange of imperishable valuables of a visible and identifiable kind.

I am also making another general point. Because social anthropologists take it for granted (sometimes mistakenly) that the distinction between true-kin and affines is of absolutely central importance they expect to find that the behaviour that is appropriate between affines will be a kind of coded inversion of the behaviour that is appropriate between true-kin.

Here is an example of such inversion which I myself observed in operation among the peasantry of North Central Ceylon; brothers were always rated as elder-brother/younger-brother and in a relationship of inequality and restraint, whereas brothers-in-law always treated one another as equals and were in a relationship of joking familiarity.

But most readers of this book will have grown up in a society in which the major comparable distinction is between kin and non-kin, and in which it is assumed, or even insisted upon, that kin relationships ought not to enter into the non-kin sphere at all. Nepotism, though of widespread occurrence, is formally considered to be an offence against common morality. So perhaps you feel that while all this talk about kinship and affinity may make good sense in discussions of the social life of Australian Aborigines or of Trobriand Islanders in Melanesia, it really has very little relevance for ourselves who live in a social context in which, as a general rule, affinity is of little significance and the majority of social relationships outside the domestic family are coded in quite a different way. But all the way through this chapter I have been asserting just the contrary.

The wage-money economy of capitalist society gives the

illusion that relationships in this kind of system are quite different in kind from those which are encountered in more 'elementary' systems. And there is a long tradition in sociological thinking which makes precisely this distinction. Henry Maine's insistence that there is a radical distinction between the *status* relationships of early, kinship-based, societies and the *contract* relationships of 'modern' societies goes back to the 1860s.[2]

De Tocqueville made a similar point even earlier when commenting on the individualizing consequences of American democracy: 'Aristocracy had made a chain of all the members of the community, from the peasant to the king: democracy breaks that chain and severs every link of it . . .'[3] And in a similar vein Marx argued that wage payments in the capitalist system had the effect of alienating the worker from the products of his labour and reducing both to the status of commodities in the market place.

But capitalist society is nothing like as fragmented and individualistic as both its admirers and its detractors would like to believe. In practice, the egalitarian individual always occupies a position in a well-defined hierarchy, and this position is repeatedly asserted by the way he behaves towards others and by the way the others react in response. The 'language' in which these assertions are made is only special in that it uses money as a social indicator where the corresponding symbolism of other economic systems might use something quite different.

As an Englishman I express my subordination to the political authority under which I live by paying a certain fraction of my money income to the appropriate official. When a Kachin householder makes a present to his local chief of the right hindleg of every animal he kills, he is 'saying' the same thing.

The fact that in capitalist society money can be used in all sorts of different exchange situations gives it a specious advantage over other media of exchange. In the eyes of professional economists barter is primitive, money currency sophisticated. And this perhaps is true where trading efficiency is the issue. But if money payments are being used to express the quality of a relationship, the symbolic possibilities are rather limited. You can pay money or not pay money; you can pay more or you can pay less; you can make payments more frequently or less frequently. But that is about all. And that is one of the reasons why, in contemporary Britain, the 'fringe benefits' which attach to a job, which are paid in kind rather than money, e.g. the use of a company car, are often of greater concern to the recipient than the precise quantity of the money wage. The fringe benefit is visible; it gives status; it differentiates. The money wage just puts you into a particular sub-section of the general category 'wage-earner'. And who wants to be that?

But, in the exchanges which are encountered by field-working anthropologists, the variety is far greater. Gift-giving can 'say' many more things and with much greater precision. I give you food. But what sort of food? Is it cooked or uncooked? Is it meat or not meat? Is it the meat of a buffalo, or a pig, or a chicken? If it is the meat of a buffalo, what precise part of the animal does it come from? A hind leg? The neck? The ribs? The liver? And so on almost *ad infinitum*. By the time I had finished my Kachin fieldwork I had only to attend an animal sacrifice as a passive observer and then notice how the meat of the sacrifice was shared out among the congregation and I could know, even down to quite fine detail, the precise hierarchy and mutual relation-ship of everyone present, which might be thirty or more individuals altogether.

But here I am once again running into the kind of

difficulty that I noted at the end of my last chapter when I quoted Christine Hugh-Jones' apposite phrase about the work of the social anthropologist being a matter of sorting out the meaning of a 'muddling mass' of detailed data. Detailed data takes up space so it cannot be presented in a volume of this scale; yet without it much of the theorizing of social anthropologists seems trivial and obvious or merely boastful. Yet to convince you that the claim I have made in my last paragraph is justifiable would require a full-length monograph at least as long as my *Political Systems of Highland Burma* which is itself a fair-sized and relevant monograph entirely devoted to the affairs of the Kachin.

So where do we go from here? I am very conscious that snippets of ethnography used to 'illustrate' an argument are often highly misleading. But I now need to make the point (among others) that it is the details that matter. So in parts of the next chapter you will be getting quite a lot of detail.

6   Marriage, Legitimacy, Alliance

I am now in something of a dilemma. I keep on insisting that customary behaviour only makes sense if it is viewed in context against a background of contrast. Up to a point I have been able to illustrate this theme by drawing attention to contrasts which are likely to be familiar to all my readers, e.g. the difference in modern Western societies between monetary and non-monetary exchanges.

But I also keep on emphasizing that the subject matter of social and cultural anthropology is the enormous diversity of customary behaviour world-wide. This diversity is interesting because it exhibits the creative originality of human beings.

Human beings must everywhere produce and reproduce both themselves and their means of subsistence, and they must also find the means to communicate with one another not just with language but through the coding that is built into the reciprocities that manifest relationship. The astonishing peculiarity of human beings, as distinct from other animals, is the great variety of ways in which they achieve these ends. My difficulty, however, is not just to show you that this is the case but rather to show you just what is the case!

What interests me as a social anthropologist is not just that human beings behave in a lot of different unexpected ways but that the patterning of these differences of behaviour also varies; and it is the continuities and the variations in these underlying patterns which are the real focus of my interest. For it is the patterning rather than the superficial form of social behaviour which conveys meaning.

As it turns out not only do we find similar 'meanings' coded into quite different formal behaviours but we also find that superficially similar formal behaviours may be coded to 'say' quite different things. This exhibits the powers of the human imagination but it is not at all easy to demonstrate in a book of this size.

Let me try to explain what I am getting at. First of all human behaviour serves both to 'do' things and to 'say' things.

By 'doing' things I mean it alters the state of the world; this is more or less what Engels had in mind with his references to production and reproduction. But Engels missed the point that human productive activity is not confined to producing the means of subsistence and the tools that go with it and to reproducing the human species itself; there is also the crucial activity of altering the social world by creating new social relationships. And in this book that is the main kind of 'doing' behaviour which is being discussed.

By 'saying' things I do not mean simply that men talk about what they do, but that all their social behaviour is 'coded' so that it makes statements about what the social situation is and where the actor is positioned in that social situation. A lot of our discussion so far has been concerned with this kind of 'saying', but I have purposely avoided introducing any of the technical jargon of semiotics (the theory of signs) and this is now leading me into difficulty because the ordinary use of words in social anthropological discourse is crudely imprecise.

Social anthropologists employ comparatively few technical terms which do not form part of the ordinary colloquial language to which they have been accustomed since childhood. We can infer from this that when the authors concerned start out to describe the institutions of an alien exotic social system they are using their own society as a model of normality. By using words which originated in the context of their own society they imply that the institutions of that society have some kind of privileged universality.

A striking example of this attitude was provided by the academic debate which took place during the early 1950s as to whether the English words 'family' and 'marriage' represented 'universal' human institutions.

Those who gave a positive answer to the question of universality seem to have arrived at their position through the following sequence of essentially functionalist propositions:

1. Human children, if they are to survive and become adults, must be cared for by adults at least until adolescence.

2. Because of this biological necessity all human societies must have rules which establish the legitimacy of young children as members of a caring domestic unit. The status of legitimacy puts obligations on the members of the domestic unit to provide care for the child. Marriage is the institution which establishes the status of legitimacy.

3. In ordinary circumstances, in the principal English-speaking societies, this caring environment is provided by a domestic household the core membership of which is a single nuclear family of married parents and children. (This ideal model does not correspond to the facts. As we all know large numbers of children in Western societies are reared in domestic households which do not have this simplistic structure at all. But this discrepancy was not brought into the discussion.)

4. The debate generally proceeded from the assumption

that the word 'family' has this restricted meaning. It was then argued, in effect, that since 'the family' (in this sense) is a functionally useful institution it must also be a necessary institution.

Most of the debate was really about an alleged universality of the nuclear family of married biological parents and their legitimate children. However when the protagonists of the universalist position got into difficulties with the ethnographic evidence they tended to evade the issue by using the word 'family' in some quite different sense! They also produced all-embracing 'definitions of marriage' of enormous complexity, the sole purpose of which was to ensure that, no matter what the ethnographic facts might be, there must always be some institution which an anthropologist could feel justified in labelling 'marriage'.

This is not just a quibble over words. Anthropologists of all kinds are greatly concerned to understand just what, if anything, is *universally* true of human society. From a biological point of view all men are very much alike; they all have very similar biological needs which must somehow be satisfied by the institutional arrangements of society. But that does not mean that the particular institutional arrangements of a particular society (namely that which provides the normal context for the use of modern English) can serve as a paradigm for all others. The form of human institutions is not determined by their functional adequacy in the way that both Malinowski and Radcliffe-Brown seem to have believed.

The general drift of my own argument, which in some ways resembles that of Marx, is that what is *determined* is not the form of particular institutional arrangements but certain basic patterns within the structure of person-to-person relationships. In any particular economic system the same patterns will be found to recur in many different social contexts within many different kinds of institution. That is why customary behaviours seem to make sense both to the actors concerned and to the anthropological observer. But the relation of pattern to form is problematic and that is what I find interesting.

It follows from this that any anthropologist who selects a particular category word from his own mother tongue, e.g. incest, marriage, family, myth, religion, and then embarks on some kind of cross-cultural study of institutions which he lumps together under such headings, is begging all the questions which are of serious interest!

Yet, on the face of it, this present chapter appears to be a cross-cultural study of 'marriage' institutions of just this sort. Appearances are deceptive.

In the first place I consider only a very small, very non-random set of examples, only four of them in any detail. Secondly, although it is true that all the institutions that are discussed have been described as 'marriage' in the relevant literature, the whole point of my argument is that this very fact tends to mislead. It may be that, in a very loose, family resemblance sense, they are all institutions of the same general kind. The similarity, such as it is, is partly a matter of form, partly a matter of function, and partly a matter of what is 'said' in symbolic performance and how it is said. But the gist of my argument is that there is no single cross-cultural matrix into which these several 'marriage' institutions can all be fitted.

They cannot be dissected into elements and made the subject of a statistical tabulation in the fashion of the *Ethnographic Atlas*. Each pattern is only meaningful in its own wider context. Nevertheless by providing these several incommensurate and incomplete 'examples' I have been able, I would claim, to demonstrate some facts about the process of forging social relationships which have general rather than particular interest.

And I would make just the same kind of point about the word 'family'. I agree that it is self-evident that any viable human society which expects to perpetuate itself through procreation (rather than through some other form of recruitment) must institutionalize some means of creating an environment in which children may be reared. But to assume that this must entail domestic arrangements which an ordinary speaker of modern colloquial English would recognize under the labels 'marriage' and 'family' is a mistake.

Actually what is now taken to be the normal and basic meaning of the English word 'family' is far removed from the meaning it carried in earlier times when the economic basis of English society was different.

The Roman *familia* was a household conceived of as a corporation, the members of which were the servants (*familus* = servant) of the head of the household, the *pater familias*. It was not a kinship group in any biological sense. Prior to the nineteenth century the English word 'family' was used in just this way to denote the members of a household, especially the servants, who, in the more affluent social classes, always greatly outnumbered the inner kin-group of parents and children.

An alternative usage, which goes back at least to the seventeenth century, made 'family' a widely dispersed group of relatives, loosely linked by ties of 'blood' and affinity, but not necessarily associated with any one household. Still another set of usages leaves out the linkages through affinity. A family then consists of those descended or claiming descent from a common ancestor. In this last specification a family might include all the diverse forms of descent group, unilineal and other, which have subsequently become part of the jargon of social anthropology, e.g. lineage, patrilineage, matrilineage, personal kindred, ramage, etc.

Indeed it would appear that until quite recently it was rather unusual for the word 'family' to mean simply the nuclear family of biological parents and children. Even now most English people use the word in several different senses. For example 'the members of the family' who gather at a funeral may be related to the deceased in all sorts of different ways but the group as a whole is unlikely to be associated with any particular household or married couple.

With all this variety it becomes almost a truism to say that families exist in all kinds of human society. But it is a statement that is quite devoid of interest.

So let us go back to *marriage*.

In ordinary English usage the word 'marriage' is used in at least four distinguishable but overlapping senses to refer to:

1. The legal rights and duties *vis-à-vis* each other of 'husband' and 'wife' on the one hand and of 'wife's husband' and 'wife's child' on the other. Hence marriage provides the children of a woman with a legitimate status in society.

2. The practical arrangements by which husband, wife and children combine to form a household. For example, the phrase 'their marriage has broken up' refers to the disintegration of the domestic group rather than to the termination of contractual relations through divorce.

3. The ceremonial (wedding) through which the husband and the wife are put into legally enforceable contractual relations with one another in the first place.

4. The relationship of alliance which links the two affinally associated 'families' which are represented in the persons of the husband and the wife. At the present time the English tend to play down the significance of affinal relationships but, even so, the statement 'she has made a

good marriage' is more likely to refer to the social and financial standing of the husband's immediate kin than to the personal qualities of the husband himself.

In one form or another these different facets of the modern English concept of marriàge reappear in most of the cross-cultural examples which I shall mention later though some of the particular forms may strike you as surprising. But first you need to notice another feature of English marital arrangements which now tends to be treated as secondary even though in the past it was of central importance. The beginning of a marriage is almost always the occasion for a transfer of valuables in the form of wedding presents, marriage settlements, token gifts.

There is enormous variation in just what is transferred and in who gives what to whom. Some of the items are highly stereotyped and of symbolic rather than economic value, e.g., the wedding ring in contemporary English custom. But, as we saw earlier, the fact that a gift expresses a relationship (as a symbol) does not necessarily imply that it is not also of great economic importance for the parties concerned.

Thus in many African 'marriage' institutions, in their traditional form, the husband and his kin made substantial payments in cattle to the male kin of the bride. The payment was a symbolic expression of the legitimacy of the marriage and of the value that was attached to it. The higher the payment, the greater the honour to the bride.

From this point of view the appropriate label for the payment is Evans-Pritchard's term: 'bridewealth'. But cattle were also the principal form of economic capital in the societies concerned; the payment was a cost to the payers. From this latter angle the more usual term 'brideprice' seems appropriate. Yet it can also be highly misleading. Christian missionaries at one time tried to have brideprice payments prohibited by law on the grounds that such payments reduced the bride to the status of a chattel slave!

Those of you who have digested the argument of my last chapter will see why this is quite the reverse of what is really the case. A chattel slave is a human being reduced to the status of a commodity in the market. The price that is paid is once for all; there is a transfer of ownership; the new owner has no enduring relationship with the previous owner. The characteristic of a chattel slave is that he(she) has no recognized kin who have continuing rights and obligations by virtue of their kinship. But a bride is of the opposite status.

African bridewealth 'marriage' establishes an enduring relationship between the husband and his kin on the one side and the bride and her kin on the other. Brideprice (bridewealth) payments are very seldom made over all at once. Usually it is a matter of payment by instalments with intervening reciprocities in the form of hospitality and counter-gifts meanwhile. The enduring relationship is treated as a perpetual debt and is made manifest from time to time by continued gift-giving throughout the duration of the marriage.

As was the case with my more general argument about gift exchange, the two aspects of the transaction, the economic and the symbolic, need to be distinguished. From the symbolic point of view it doesn't really matter very much in which direction the marriage valuables flow. Lévi-Strauss' thesis that marriage is always a contractual arrangement between groups of males and that the principal valuable in marriage is always the bride herself would imply that, on balance, the other valuables, e.g. cattle, jewellery, money, ritual objects, should move from the wife-takers to the wife-givers. But this pattern is not always borne out by the ethnographic evidence.

There are cases where, from an economic point of view, the marriage valuables represent the purchase of a husband by the bride rather than vice versa, and the general European pattern, which is met with in many other parts of the world, is for the principal payment to be the bride's 'dowry', a set of assets which she brings with her into the marriage as a part of her inheritance from her own kin. One of the important variables in such patterns is the degree to which the dowry assets remain exclusively the property of the bride herself and of *her* future heirs or become a part of the pool of household property which can be used by the husband. In many such systems the size of the gift is widely publicized within the local community; here once again the greater the size of the gift, the greater the honour to the bride.

And here is one further general point before we start to consider particular examples. Many of the confusions in the anthropological literature arise from the failure to make an adequate distinction between biological relationship and socially recognized relationship. Standard textbooks of anthropology usually adopt some version of the formula: 'Marriage is a union between a man and a woman such that the children of a woman are the recognized legitimate offspring of both partners'.[1] It is obvious that such a definition is defective even within the context of ordinary English usuage. Many English marriages are infertile but this does not invalidate the marriage. Moreover married couples, whether fertile or infertile may adopt children who are not the biological offspring of either partner and such children are then considered to be the 'legitimate offspring of both parents'.

As you will see, definitions of this type fit very badly with the institutions that I shall presently describe. In most cases the discrepancy arises because 'legitimacy' (a social concept) is not tied in with the issue of who is the biological parent of the child.

The rules concerning the possibility of adoption vary very greatly. Some societies insist that the only genuine relationship between parent and child is the bond established by biology. But such systems are exceptional. To suppose, as Lévi-Strauss and others have done, that rules about *exogamy* – 'those we may not marry' – and rules about *incest* – 'those with whom we may not have sexual intercourse' – directly match up, so that one kind of rule can serve as an explanation for the other, is an ethnographic mistake. My first example, which is very well-known, exemplifies this point as well as a number of the other themes which I have been discussing. From now on I will use the term 'marriage' simply to denote the institution immediately under discussion without prejudging the issue as to whether the different kinds of 'marriage' thus presented are or are not members of a single logical class.

Case 1. The Nuer (Southern Sudan)[2]

The Nuer are transhumant cattle breeders. They are organized in segmentary patrilineal lineages. A contract of marriage entails the transfer of bridecattle from the husband to the male next-of-kin of the wife. By virtue of the transfer of cattle the woman's biological offspring are ordinarily deemed to be members of the descent group of the husband rather than that of the woman's father; payment of the cattle makes the children legitimate; cohabitation alone does not.

Normally the husband is a living man who is both the original owner of the cattle and also the actual biological father (*genitor*) of the woman's children, but in exceptional circumstances the bridecattle may derive from a deceased bridegroom or from a woman owner of cattle. In either case the original owner of the bridecattle rates as the 'father' of the children of the bride. The identity of the *genitor* in such cases is largely irrelevant.

The arrangement by which a young man, who dies before he is married, can nevertheless marry and have descendants (provided always that he was the owner of cattle) is rather similar to the biblical institution of the *levirate*, but the elaboration which allows a woman to become a legal 'father' at first seems more peculiar. It is however perfectly logical.

The Nuer legal fiction is that only men can be the owners of cattle. However, if a man dies without direct male heirs, his cattle will be inherited by a daughter. This cattle-owning daughter is then a sociological male. She can (and should) marry a wife so as to perpetuate her deceased father's lineage. The wife (whom she marries with bridecattle in the ordinary way) cohabits with an unspecified outsider, but when the wife becomes pregnant the *genitor* has no legal standing *vis-à-vis* the prospective child. The child's legal father is the woman who paid the mother's bridecattle.

The main point about this example was to show that social roles which speakers of English would ordinarily assume to be alternative titles for the same individual, e.g., 'father', 'husband', 'begetter of wife's children', are not only distinguishable but may be distributed in quite unexpected ways. This same point about the divisibility of roles which are ordinarily assumed to be interchangeable is further exemplified by my second example which is another piece of classic ethnography.

Case 2. The 'traditional' Nayar (Kerala State, South India)[3]

The Nayar form the dominant cultivator caste in central Kerala. At the present time their marriage practices are not very different from those of their neighbours though there is considerable diversity in different sections of the community. The 'classical' account, which is summarized below, refers to an eighteenth- rather than a twentieth-century political context.

At that period many of the younger Nayar males were likely to be away from home for long periods of military service. The royal families of the local principalities were Nayar but many of the major landlords were Brahmins of the Nambudiri caste. In ritual status they were at the very top of the system and ranked higher even than the kings. The role of the Nambudiri in the Kerala of that period was rather similar to that of the Catholic church in the Holy Roman Empire of medieval Europe.

The Nambudiri were organized in patrilineal lineages; the Nayar in localized matrilineages known as *taravad*. *Taravad* also denoted the farmstead/joint household of the members of the matrilineage.

In a formal sense a Nayar *taravad* was the matrilineal equivalent of the patrilineal joint family homestead that is to be encountered in many parts of rural India but with the peculiarity that the incoming spouses (i.e., the 'husbands' of the locally domiciled women) had no legal standing.

With rare exceptions complete authority over the affairs and property of the *taravad* lay with the eldest male, the *karanavan*. The other residents who had legal standing were the sisters and younger brothers of the *karanavan*, and the children of the sisters and of the sisters' daughters. The *genitors* of the children had a recognized standing in relation to their spouses but they visited them only at night and did not take food in the *taravad* house of their 'wives'. Even this limited access needed the approval of the *karanavan*. Although the *genitor*-lover had no legal or economic rights there were certain public festivals when he would publicly make small token gifts to his 'wife' as evidence that he intended the relationship to continue.

The term used to denote the relationship between the girl and her lover was *sambandham* which in other parts of South India denotes 'marriage' of a more straighforward kind. It is also the ordinary word for 'marriage' in modern Nayar communities where property-owning has become individualized and most of the traditional *taravad* homesteads have disappeared. A girl could have a number of *sambandham* lovers, either at the same time or in sequence. They could never be of lower caste than herself and the principle of lineage exogamy applied. The relationship was initiated or terminated with minimal ceremony though it could endure for a lifetime. A woman's children addressed the man who was supposed to be their *genitor* by a term which means 'father' in neighbouring communities.

Despite this seeming laxity in sexual affairs the Nayar drew a sharp distinction between the status of an unmarried girl and a mother. It was highly reprehensible for a young girl who had not been properly initiated into the status of motherhood to become pregnant.

The normal procedure was that, at an elaborate ritual (the *tali*-tying ceremony) which had to be held before her first menstruation, every girl was 'married' to a ritual husband who came from a matrilineage which had the status of *enangar* in relation to her own. The *enangar* linkages between Nayar matrilineages provided a permanent chain of affinity which linked together all the lineages of similar standing within a neighbourhood. The relationship was made manifest at the life crisis ceremonials of partner lineages.

An *enangar* lineage had to provide representatives to attend the naming ceremony of a baby, the first rice feeding in the sixth month, the pre-puberty 'marriage' rite of girls, the first menstruation rite of a girl, the first pregnancy ceremony of a woman, and on various occasions connected with mortuary rites and death pollution.

The third of these occasions is the most immediately relevant. Each lineage had to provide suitable young men to act as 'husbands' (*enangan*) in the *tali*-tying ceremonials of their *enangar* which were grand collective affairs held every ten years or so for all the immature girls of the group. Each such 'pre-puberty marriage' lasted three days and nights during which period the couple was secluded together in a room in the ancestral house. The 'marriage' was then terminated by formal divorce. The *enangan* had no subsequent special rights either in the girl or in her future children though her children addressed him by a title used as a respectful term for 'Father' among some neighbouring groups. They also had special duties to fulfil at his funeral.

In this case, in contrast to the informal arrangements between an adult girl and her *sambandham* lover, both the 'marriage' (the *tali*-tying ceremony) and the 'divorce' (the cloth-tearing ceremony) were grand public performances. Their symbolic significance was also very plain. The *tali*-tying is a shared feature of most South Indian weddings: the torn cloth showed that the 'marriage' was at an end.

There is one further feature of the ethnography which must be mentioned before I discuss the general pattern. In the patrilineal extended families of the Nambudiri landlord aristocrats only the eldest son was allowed to marry with full

Vedic rites so as to produce legitimate children. This limitation prevented the continuous fragmentation of the patrimonial estate. But although the younger sons could not have Nambudiri wives it was quite normal and respectable for them to take women of the matrilineal castes (e.g. Nayar) as recognized consorts.

In Nambudiri eyes these women were concubines; therefore the children belonged to the mother's caste not to the father's caste. But, from the Nayar point of view, all children belong to the mother's caste anyway and hypergamous unions of this kind were highly prestigious. The children were treated as fully legitimate members of the mother's *taravad.*

I have given this Nayar material at some length because it exemplifies such a large number of the themes which I have been emphasizing throughout this book. Let me draw your attention to some of these features.

If you are interested, as I am, in the symbolic representation of relationships then you must pay close attention both to contrast and to small details. In stressing the insecure, non-legal standing of the *sambandham* husband Nayar informants told the ethnographers that the *sambandham* partner never took food in the house of his 'wife'.

The point here is that, in this cultural context, publicly recognized commensality is an index of a relatively permanent bond of relationship.

The complementary contrast is provided by a detail from my own fieldwork experience in North Central Sri Lanka where, despite the absence of any form of lineage organization, much of the ideology concerning marriage is very similar to that encountered in Kerala.

In the Sri Lankan situation 'marriages' were distinguished according to whether they were *diga* (virilocal – wife goes to her husband's house) or *binna* (uxorilocal – husband goes to his wife's house). The marriage in both cases was described as *sambandham* but, in the latter, the status of the husband was precarious and often very temporary. When I tried to discover just what was really meant when it was said of a particular girl that she had been 'married' in this sense seven times before she was nineteen, I was told that if a girl was seen to be cooking a meal for a man this was evidence that she was 'married' to him.

The Nayar case also illustrates my earlier comments on the anthropologists' use of the term 'society' and of their attempts to set up typologies of societies of various kinds. One of the very earliest of these schemes, which has shown exceptional survival value because of its adoption by orthodox Marxists, was the postulate that 'matrilineal societies' form a class distinct from 'patrilineal societies' and that, in the world scale history of social evolution, the former have always preceded the latter.

However in the Nayar case it is clear that the matrilineal organization of the Nayar *taravad* only makes sense when it is viewed as a part of the larger society which included the patrilineal organization of the Nambudiri and the military organization of the pre-British South Indian principalities. It is this larger system, considered as a whole, which is functionally integrated and which was able to reproduce itself within a framework of legitimacy despite the absence on military service of many of the potential *genitors* of the children. Matriliny and patriliny are thus complementary rather than contrasted principles and we shall entirely miss the point if we treat the Nambudiri and the Nayar as belonging to different 'types' of society.

Another of my themes that is well illustrated by the Nayar material is that the structure of society consists of a network of implicit rights and obligations which link together not only individuals (considered as social persons) but also larger groups such as households and village communities. There is also the supplementary point that very commonly the 'we'-groups that are thus linked together treat their solidarity as deriving from common substance, in contrast to the alliances, which link 'we' and 'they', which rest on obligations periodically expressed in gift-giving and services.

In the Nayar case the solidarity of the members of a *taravad* is one of common substance. They are descended from a common ancestress through female links only and they have been nurtured on food which derives from a common parcel of land. On the other hand the links which tie the different *taravad* together through the *enangar* network, and the links which bond the Nayar to their Nambudiri superiors, are ties of permanent indebtedness which have the characteristics of perpetual affinity. This is despite the fact that all the more straightforward definitions of 'marriage' fail to fit the peculiarities of the Nayar case. You will notice incidentally that whereas the *enangar* relationship can be reciprocal because the paired groups are ordinarily of the same social status, the relationship with the Nambudiri, who are of superior ritual standing, is always asymmetrical. Nambudiri men may cohabit with Nayar women; Nayar men may never cohabit with Nambudiri women.

For my next example I will go back to Sri Lanka for a case which exhibits with particular clarity the general principle that equality of status calls for direct equivalence in reciprocal behaviour.

Case 3. Traditional marriage ceremonial among upper caste Sinhalese

As with the Nayar example the following ethnography has an eighteenth- rather than a twentieth-century flavour but weddings of a similar general type can still be observed. It should be borne in mind that the material comes from the same general cultural context as the young lady who had been 'married' seven times before she was nineteen. The extreme elaboration of the proceedings is intended to emphasize that, in contrast to the kind of marriage which can be entered into or broken off on the spur of the moment, this is a contract which is intended to endure. It is an expression of alliance between groups of kin rather than a short-term arrangement between two private individuals. In this respect it is analogous to the Nayar *tali*-tying ceremony rather than to the Nayar *sambandham*, except that the bride is physically mature and the ritual husband is her real husband, the presumed *genitor* of her future children.

In the ideal case the sequence of events was as follows:

1. The groom's kin opened negotiations with the bride's kin through neutral intermediaries.

2. Friends of the groom paid a formal visit to the parents of the bride and viewed the bride herself. The visitors were treated to rice and betel.

3. A mother's brother of the groom repeated this visit and the horoscopes of the bride and bridegroom were exchanged. Provided these were compatible an auspicious day was chosen for the wedding.

4. On the appointed day the parents of the groom sent presents of betel, cakes, fruit, etc. to the parents of the bride.

5. Later the groom's party set out in three separate ceremonial processions to the home of the bride. The groom's father with attendants went first followed by the groom's mother and her attendants followed by the groom and his attendants.

6. Outside the compound of the bride's parents the processions were met by similar processional parties of near

relatives of the bride. A brother or father's brother of the bride should meet the first group; a sister or mother's sister of the bride the second group; a cross-cousin of the bride the third group. The bride's parents should not be present at this stage. (It should be noted here that the groom himself is of necessity a classifactory cross-cousin of the bride, for the rule is that all marriages must be between kinsmen of the same caste. All such kinsmen are, from a girl's point of view, either 'brothers' or 'cross-cousins' and she may not marry a 'brother'. The convention is that the cross-cousin who meets the groom's party at the gate should challenge the groom saying that he, the gatekeeper, has first claim to the girl. The groom should then pay the gatekeeper a token gift to allow the procession to pass. This piece of play acting serves to publicize the fact that the forthcoming marriage conforms to the rules of caste endogamy and 'incest' prohibitions.)

7. Between the gate and the decorated central room where the wedding ceremony would take place a ritually clean white cloth had been laid on the ground and the visitors walked on this once they were past the gate. At the same time a coconut was split in half in honour of Ganesha, the guardian of thresholds. (The symbolism of both these actions is that of a 'rite of separation' in Van Gennep's sense. The cloth marks a threshold, the boundary between the outside and the inside of a temporarily sacred precint. In Sinhalese imagery the two ends of a coconut represent respectively the penis of a man and the breasts of a woman and the preliminary separation of the two ends is appropriate at the beginning of a wedding which is to unite male and female. The same coconut rite is a feature of other Sinhalese life-crisis ceremonials, e.g. that which marks a girl's first menstruation; the way the two halves of the coconut fall is taken as an augury for the future of the marriage.)

8. As the guests stepped off the cloth into the wedding room the business of the coconut was repeated all over again.

9. In the wedding proceedings proper the mother of the groom gave a valuable cloth and jewels to the mother of the bride; the father of the bride gave a suit of splendid clothing to the groom. At an auspicious moment the groom threw a gold chain over the bride's neck and presented her with a wedding dress and jewels.

10. The bride and the groom, now dressed in their new clothes, stood together on a plank covered with a white cloth which was described as a 'seed harrow' (*poruva*).

11. A mother's brother of the bride then tied the little finger of the bride's right hand to the little finger of the groom's left hand with a gold chain. They rotated three times on the plank and the chain was removed. (When Sinhalese thresh their paddy, pairs of buffaloes yoked together are walked round and round the threshing floor at night. However the seemingly obvious agricultural reference of the symbolism of the marriage *poruva* and the rotation of the chained couple was not explicitly recognized by my Pul Eliya informants.)

12. The bride and the groom ate from the same dish. In Sinhalese imagery this has a quite explicit connotation of sexual intercourse.

13. There was general feasting by the assembled guests.

14. A mixed party of kin from both sides, including the bride and the gatekeeper cross-cousin but not the bride's parents, returned in procession to the house of the groom's parents. At the gate they were met by a close cross-cousin of the groom. The two cross-cousins exchanged greetings and token presents. The business of splitting a coconut was repeated. After being entertained to food the bride's kin departed.

15. The young couple were now secluded together for a week in a specially decorated apartment.

16. On the seventh day the bride's mother's brother, who had performed the original *poruva* ceremony, together with his wife and other relatives of the bride (not her parents) arrived in procession.

17. The bridal couple again stood on a *poruva*, this time with their heads covered. Two new pots were filled with water. In each pot was placed a gold coin by a representative of the groom who also gave a gold ring to the bride's mother's brother. At an auspicious moment the latter poured the water over the heads of the bridal couple. Their head covering was then removed. (A very similar performance occurs in the concluding stages of a variety of Sinhalese rituals. The water is intended to wash away the contamination of sacredness of persons who have been acting a priestly role. If they were not washed in this way they would be a danger to their neighbours on returning to ordinary secular activities. The potency of such sacredness is supposed to be an emanation from the eyes; hence the covering of the head. In the case of a bridal couple the ideology is that during the initiatory phase of their marriage the groom and his bride are playing out the roles of a god and a goddess; when they resume their life as ordinary mortals their dangerous divinity must be removed.)

18. After further feasting the visitors from the bride's home departed.

19. After an interval of several weeks there were further exchange visits between the two households. First the bride's parents with attendants visited the newly married couple in their home; then after a further interval the married couple made a similar formal visit to the bride's parents. It was only at this stage that the dowry of the bride, which would usually have included both jewels and the title deeds to land, was

actually handed over by the bride's parents though details of the dowry would have been settled right at the beginning at Stage 1 of the proceedings.

20. Apart from the various gifts of valuables and food and clothing which marked the exchanges between the principles, there were also certain standard payments *in money* which were made to the washerman who prepared the cloths used at various stages in the proceedings. The groom paid this money fee to the washerman who decorated the house of the bride's parents; the cross-cousin of the bride paid the fee of the washerman who decorated the house of the groom's parents. The astrologers who determined the various 'auspicious moments' mentioned in my account would also have received a fee, though in what form and from whom I do not know.

From this lengthy account the balanced reciprocity which I mentioned at the beginning becomes very clear but some of you may think that the detail is excessive. My justification is that the details illustrate a number of quite general anthropological themes which are important quite outside the context of this particular case.

First I should explain that my account is a combination of a statement made around 1826 by a Kandyan aristocrat in reply to an enquiry from the British agent Sir John D'Oyly and of material which I recorded myself in Sri Lanka in 1954. The high degree of congruence between the two sets of materials shows that D'Oyly's informant was reciting a well-established stereotype. My alterations to D'Oyly's account in fact amount to little more than replacing 'kinsman of the bride', 'kinsman of the bridegroom' by 'mother's brother' or 'cross-cousin' as appropriate.

The wedding which I observed at first hand in 1954 in the peasant community of Pul Eliya was nothing like as grand as the stereotype; but, apart from some minor differences, it had all the same elements and for the most part they occurred in just the same sequence. This is very much what I would have expected. Nevertheless the degree to which custom, as directly observed, conforms or does not conform to a predetermined stereotype needs to be looked at very carefully.

If, as a fieldworker, you record the 'same' myth on two separate occasions, it is very likely that, at first sight, the two versions will appear entirely different. Yet on closer inspection it will be found that they both contain just the same structural components. The constituent units may be of quite different length and they may appear in quite a different order and quite different emphases may be given to particular features of the story, but the corpus as a whole will contain the same set of elements.

And so also with ritual performances of all kinds. If the anthropologist enquires in advance about just what is going to happen, his informants will give him a stereotype. When he observes the actual performance he may find it difficult to associate what he has seen with what he had been led to expect. Yet enquiry will show that everything in fact happened just as predicted. It is simply that a feature, which seemed prominent in the stereotype, may appear insignificant in the performance, and vice versa.

Ritual sequences such as the Sinhalese wedding described above are made up of units which are used rather like the pieces in a game of dominoes. The units are put together to form meaningful chains of symbolism but the same units may turn up in quite different ritual contexts.

For example, in the case of the Pul Eliya wedding, I was not around to witness the business of pouring water over the veiled faces of the bride and bridegroom which I was told would take place and which is included in D'Oyly's 1828 account. However, in the same Pul Eliya context, the business of the two pots with the gold coins formed part of the procedure for bringing a spirit medium out of his state of possession, while the business of the head shroud worn by an individual in a state of dangerous sanctity occurred in an elaborate ritual for the painting of the eyes of a new image of the Lord Buddha.

The artist who painted in the eyes gave power to the image but was in turn filled with dangerous emanations which had to be washed off before he could return to ordinary life. He therefore came out of the temple walking backwards with his whole head covered by a cloth and immediately dipped his head in a basin of water before removing the covering.

The point I am making here is that the interpretation of symbolic action in the context of social relations is not just a matter of inspired hunch. The logic of the exercise becomes apparent when we observe how the same behavioural detail is used in *different* ritual contexts.

But what do we mean by *same* in such an argument? We are concerned with the quality of relationships as expressed by contrasts rather than with a direct concordance of ethnographic fact. At the manifest level of observable facts, the differences may be as significant as the similarities. In the case of mythology the saga teller will always produce a version of the story which puts his own ancestors in a particularly favourable light. In the case of ritual performance the details sometimes vary simply because the actors have forgotten what ought to happen next! But differences may also reflect special features in the local situation.

For example, in the case of the wedding ceremony, one of the small ways in which Pul Eliya practice differed from the aristocratic schema described by D'Oyly was that, in Pul Eliya, the washermen were not paid in money but in grain paddy at the end of the year.

The washermen in this system are members of the Hena caste and their caste function is the handling of ritually polluted objects and the provision of ritually clean clothes and pieces of cloth. Because of their association with pollution they rate 'low' in the caste hierarchy. Sexual relations between a Hena and a Goigama (the cultivator caste of the inhabitants of Pul Eliya) would be considered horrifying. Nevertheless the Hena villagers, in their ordinary lives, led much the same sort of existence as the Goigama villagers. In any particular case the link between the Goigama household and the Hena household was permanent and at a personal level relations could be quite close. The Goigama paid their Hena 'retainers' in a formal gift-giving once a year. The gift took the form of uncooked food, usually paddy.

Two contrasts are involved here. Gift exchange between fellow Goigama ordinarily took the form of cooked food. Paddy would only change hands as part of a specific economic debt contracted outside the field of kinship relations. On the other hand when the Goigama made *money* payments in return for services or labour it was always to people who were right outside the system such as shopkeepers or Tamil labourers hired on a casual basis.

The fact that D'Oyly's aristocratic informant said that the washermen should be paid for their service with money (*ridi*) may simply reflect the greater social distance which separated the aristocrats from the Hena, or it could be that, at that date, the distinction between commercial and non-commercial economic transactions had not yet become so clear-cut as it is today. But D'Oyly's informant still insisted on a difference in kind as between transactions within the caste, that is with kin, and transactions with members of another caste, that is with non-kin. This is fully in accord with what I have said about the expression of 'we'/'they' oppositions in other contexts.

The Sinhalese wedding case also has general value because it provides an exceptionally clear example of the three-phase structure of rites of passage first recognized by Hertz and Van Gennep around 1908[4] but which has subsequently been shown to apply to all kinds of social rituals.

The general point is that, in terms of direct experience, the progress of biological time and the distribution of territorial space are continuous. There is no precise moment or position at which one can say of a particular individual that the child has become an adult or that the man who was outside the house is now inside. But in social time and social space we make just such distinctions and we do so in a very consistent way.

The social person first moves out of his original position (role) ('the rite of separation'); he then exists for a time in a liminal condition, a threshold of time and space which is outside the ordinary world of secular affairs and is treated as in some way 'sacred' (Van Gennep's '*rite de marge*'); finally he moves back into secular society in his new position (role) ('the rite of aggregation').

In the first and the third of these phases, roles and statuses are carefully distinguished; in the second they are confused, 'we' and 'they' are mixed up, behaviour which would be outrageous in ordinary life becomes normal and even obligatory.

In my Sinhalese wedding example, phases 1–5 constitute the rite of separation; phases 6–15 the '*rite de marge*'; 16–20 the rite of aggregation. Read through the material again and work out for yourself just how closely this three-phase pattern matches that of some 'rite of passage' which you know directly from first-hand experience such as a wedding

or a funeral or an initiation/investiture of any kind
whatsoever.

But we must move on. I want now to consider some
further aspects of 'the creation of legitimacy' which most
anthropologists consider to be *the* crucial function of any
institution described as 'marriage'. Our examples do not fit
with this formula. In Case 1 we saw how the Nuer linked
legitimacy to the payment of bridecattle; in Case 2 Nayar
legitimacy was established by the child's mother being of the
proper social age, a 'mother' and not a 'child', with the added
proviso that the presumed *genitor* must not be of lower caste
than the mother. But the initiation of a virgin girl into the
status of 'mother' was a 'marriage' only in symbol. By
contrast, in Case 3, all Sinhalese children are legitimate
members of society provided that the presumed *genitor* is not
of lower caste than the mother. 'Marriage', however defined,
is not a relevant factor at all.

The dowry of a wife married by formal contract, which
moves from the wife's kin to the husband's household,
affects the economic prospects of the woman's future
children (since they will all have rights in the property of
both their acknowledged parents) but is does not affect their
legitimacy. This is important. Dowry payment in the
Sinhalese style is not just the obverse of the Nuer bridecattle
which move from the husband's kin to the wife's kin.

But leaving dowry aside, how far is it true that payments
of brideprice (bridewealth) from the husband's kin to the
wife's kin always serve to 'legitimize the children of the
marriage'? As usual the answer is not straightforward.

Case 4. The North Burma Kachin

The Kachin are for the most part slash and burn cultivators of hill paddy. They have a segmentary patrilineal lineage system which is, in some respects, similar to that of the Nuer (Case 1). A major difference is that the Kachin lineage segments are ranked into a class hierarchy: chiefs, aristocrats, commoners (slaves). In times past the village community often consisted of just a single longhouse inhabited by the male members of a single patrilineage segment and their wives and children. A schematic lay-out of such a longhouse is shown in Figure 6.1 which is referred to opposite.

The Kachin feature prominently in contemporary anthropological literature because Lévi-Strauss made them his type case for a society in which marriage functions as a system of generalized exchange and because of various writings of my own.

The asymmetrical aspect of Kachin marrige is certainly very fundamental. The 'wife-givers' (*maya ni*), i.e. the patrilineage of the wife, and the 'wife-receivers' (*dama ni*), i.e., the patrilineage of the husband, are considered to be bonded in a semi-permanent alliance which affects every aspect of the structure of society, but I am concerned here only with the issue of legitimacy.

In traditional Kachin society prenuptial sexual intercourse was institutionalized. The unmarried girls of the longhouse were allocated a special room (16 in Fig. 6.1) in which they might sleep with their lovers. Nevertheless it was considered disgraceful if an 'unmarried' girl, i.e., a girl for whom no one had yet paid, or arranged to pay bridewealth, bore a child. Such a child was a 'bastard' (*nji*) and rated initially as a low status member of its mother's patrilineage.

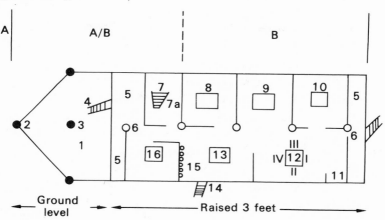

1. Covered porch and stable—*n'pan*. 2. Front house post—*jun shadaw*. 3. Porch house post—*n'hpu daw*. 4. Entrance ladder —*lakang*. 5. Verandah—*n'tawt*. 6. Door—*chyinghka*. 7. Madai nat shrine room—*madai dap*. 7a. Madai shrine—*karap tawn*. 8,9,10,12,13,16. Hearths—*dap*. 8. Hearth of married son's family—*lapran dap*. 9. Hearth of householder's young children and servants. 10. Sleeping quarters of householder—*n'bang dap*. 11. Shrine of household *nat-nat tawn*. 12. Guest hearth—*manam dap, lup daw dap*. There is an order of precedence as to seating position indicated by the figures I, II, III, IV. 13. Cooking hearth—*shat shadu dap*. 14. Side entrance—*hkuwawt hku*. 15. Rack for water tubes—*ntsin n'dum*. 16. Private room of unmarried adolescent girls—*n-la dap*.

Figure 6.1: Schematic layout of Kachin Longhouse

If the mother named a putative father this created a 'debt' (*hka*) between the lineage of the girl and the lineage of the man so named. If the girl was of high standing and the man refused to accept responsibility, the debt could develop into a major feud, but otherwise, if the father wished to have the child, he could pay a fine of ten 'items' (*hpaga*), eight of which went to the girl's parents, and the other two to the girl herself.

The payment of this fine (*sumrai hka*– 'the debt of the umbilical cord') served to redeem the child but explicitly cut off any continuing tie between the two parents. The child became a legitimate member of the father's patrilineage but no *mayu/dama* alliance had been established between the mother's lineage and the father's lineage. Here then is a case where the distinctions legitimate/illegitimate and married/unmarried can both be exactly specified but the two oppositions do not match 1:1.

There are a vast variety of other things that I might say about the complex of institutions which surround Kachin marriage but I will confine myself to just one corner of this elaborate map, nearly all the details of which are directly relevant to my earlier argument.

First of all, the 'items' paid to redeem the bastard child are not just a monetary compensation. Some have 'real' economic value: the items should include a quantity of silver and two buffaloes. Others are symbolic. The girl herself receives one *hpaga* (often a cloth) 'for nursing the infant' and 'for wiping her face' and a necklace 'for the loss of her virginity'. Items paid to the parents of the girl should include a gun 'for the spinal column (of the child)', a gong 'for the body', a Chinese silk coat 'for the skin', and, most important of all, a sword 'to cut off the debt'.

Such lists of items, which are a prominent feature of Kachin custom, are stereotypes, notional ideals; in this case (redemption of a bastard child of commoner parents) the items actually paid over will always be ten in number but probably be of quite a different quality. But if a piglet is presented in lieu of a buffalo it will be described as a buffalo throughout the ceremony of presentation.

The next point to which I would draw your attention is the distinction between the girl as an individual and the patrilineage as a collective social person.

The girl's love affairs are her own business. She is provided with amenities in the form of private living space, but otherwise no questions are asked so long as she does not get pregnant. Most of her affairs are likely to be with boys whom she could not marry on grounds of 'incest', i.e. all the boys with whom she is in brother/sister or mother's brother/sister's daughter relationship, which would include all close cousins other than her *dama ni* relatives. The reason for this is that, as a rule, neither the boy nor the girl wants to get trapped into a formal marriage.

But in sharp contrast, all formal marriages involving bridewealth transactions and ceremony, are arranged between heads of lineage households through intermediaries. In this case, if the husband is a young boy, he takes no visible part in the proceedings. The head of the household will say, on the occasion of a wedding, 'We are taking a woman', *not* 'My son (or my grandson) is taking a woman'.

And that brings me back to my diagram, at the top of which I have marked off, from left to right, three zones: A, A/B, B. The residential part of the house is 3 feet or more above ground level and is entered by a ladder consisting of a notched trunk of wood. All non-resident visitors must always enter by the front ladder (4) passing through the cattle pen en route (1). This is also the porch and the post (3) is adorned with an array of cattle skulls commemorating past sacrificial feasts given by the occupants.

The front ladder (4) is always renewed on the occasion of a wedding and the new bride, carrying a basket of symbolic objects which constitute her trousseau rather than a dowry, is always the first individual to ascend the new ladder. The notches in the ladder are *hka*, the same word as 'debt', and they represent a sort of tally of the 'debts' which bind the household to their *mayu ni*, the household from which the bride has come.

Within the house the area to the right of the dotted line, which I have marked B, rates as secular public space except that the room marked '10' is the private accommodation of the household head and his wife. Diagonally opposite is '16', the semi-private room where the the adolescent girls entertain their lovers, but this is in my space A/B. Also in space A/B is room '7' which is, primarily, a shrine to a major ancestor deity associated with chieftainship.

The point of my three spatial categories is that A is fully 'outside', B is fully 'inside', A/B is 'betwixt and between' and it is in this A/B area that we find (a) the shrine to a major deity, (b) the animals which will eventually be sacrificed to this and other deities, (c) the 'private' sleeping accommodation of the adolescent girls and their unofficial lovers, (d) the ladder which symbolizes the enduring debt relationship between the *dama ni* and their *mayu ni*. Notice that the frontier between A/B and B (the 'sacred' and the 'profane') is marked by a line of drinking water containers (15). It is one of the principal tasks of the adolescent girls to keep these replenished.

Perhaps this will help you to see what I was getting at earlier on when I said that, from the social anthropologist's point of view, the structure of kinship relationships is just one possible way of looking at patterns which also crop up in the spatial arrangements of buildings, in areas of economics, and in the cosmology which links the land of the living to the land of the ancestral dead.

If however you are unpersuaded and feel that the lay-out of a Kachin longhouse has not the remotest relevance to anything in which you might be interested, may I suggest that you draw a groundplan of the house or flat where you are now living.

Mark on it the entrances, the latrines, the bathrooms, the cooking places, the eating places, the spaces where guests are entertained, the bedrooms. And then reflect on the fact that in English culture these different kinds of space are differentiated as 'private' or 'public' in several cross-cutting ways. Note further that the underlying basis of such differentiation relates to eating/defecation, clean/dirty, cooked/uncooked, sexual relations/asexual relations, inside/outside, etc.

Of course the ethnography is very different. The English do not engage in animal sacrifice; they do not think of affinity as a relationship which endures through many generations. Yet at the level of patterning there are some striking similarities.

In *The Temple and the House* (1964) the late Lord Raglan maintained that we could only understand the arrangements of a typical English dwelling house if we thought of it as a temple with the marriage bed as a shrine. I fancy that most of his fellow anthropologists thought that his book was a display both of amateurism and of senility. And certainly it is an odd sort of book, but in some ways very shrewd indeed.

My two final cases will be very brief and I have introduced them partly to confuse the issue. Both are referred to in the literature as 'marriage' and one can see why; moreover, the first example is concerned with the legitimacy of children. But they raise a further red herring: What is the connection between marriage and prostitution? Although I shall not pursue that question it is not irrelevant in the present context for just as the Kachin put a halo of sacredness around the sexual promiscuity of their young women because they are socially out of control, so also prostitution and other forms of 'irregular' sexual activity which are both tolerated and not tolerated are very frequently associated with religious activity.

Case 5. Mut'a marriage (Muslim Middle East)

This is a short-term contract undertaken for the period of a pilgrimage or while a man is on a protracted business trip. The contract specifies from the start the length of time the union is to last. The man pays his 'wife' for services rendered but there are no further obligations as between the woman and the man. However, if the woman becomes pregnant and bears a child, the child is legitimate and is entitled to his or her share among other heirs of the father.

Case 6. Siwah Oasis (Western Egypt)[5]

An ethnographer writing in 1936 reported that: 'All normal Siwan men and boys practise sodomy ... Among themselves the natives are not ashamed of this; they talk about it as openly as they talk about the love of women, and many, if not most of their fights arise from homosexual competition.' Until quite recently marriages were celebrated between men and boys as well as between men and women. Marriage to a boy was celebrated with great pomp and publicity and the 'brideprice' paid for a boy might be as much as fifteen times that paid for a girl.

The last example is quite unsatisfactory because we are not told what relationships, other than the sexual one, resulted from the 'marriage'; but a variety of cases have been reported from other parts of the world in which the ongoing obligation to activate a relationship of perpetual affinity by providing a woman as a bride can be satisfied by providing a boy if no suitable girl is available.

So we come back to where we started. Words like

'marriage', 'family', 'religion' do not mean very much when viewed in a cross-cultural framework. But the patterns of relationship which turn up in the institutions which get allocated to these categories are important patterns which always invite the anthropologist's closest attention. 'Marital' relations in particular, in providing a bridge between the biological and the social, serve to illuminate in a very special way the manner in which the local population has resolved the paradoxes which arise from our attempts to fit the continuity of nature to the discontinuities of social categories.

7　Some Aspects of Cosmology

Let me remind you again of Christine Hugh-Jones' remark about the anthropologist having to piece together his model of the social structure from a 'muddling mass' of informants' statements (p. 147). There the argument was that the dimension of kinship (in the broad sense used by the social anthropologist) and the dimension of cosmology (as talked about by the anthropologist's informants) were transform-ations of each other, so that any argument about how things are or should be can take either form. This is a very general situation.

As we saw right at the beginning of Chapter 1, modern anthropologists can, according to their inclination, specialize in all sorts of different aspects of the way of life of the people they have chosen to study, and I certainly would not want to argue that there is any specially 'correct' way of sorting out the muddling mass of data with which the fieldworker is faced, but, in my experience, a vulgar Marxist approach to the problem has certain merits, at least as a starting point.

The basis of everything, the 'infrastructure', is the mode of subsistence and the organization of labour that goes with it. At the other extreme is the cosmology, the ideological 'superstructure', which serves as a justification for every-thing that goes on. And in between, but permeating both, is the dimension of kinship.

My book about the Kachin, *Political Systems of Highland*

Burma (1954), was about kinship in the frame of ideology; my book about Sinhalese peasants, *Pul Eliya: A Village in Ceylon* (1961), was about kinship as an expression of economic relationships. You can play it either way, or in some quite different way. But that is how it seems to me; the data present themselves to the enquiring anthropologist in three interlocking dimensions: economy, kinship, cosmology (or if you prefer it 'religion').

The study of the economy is particular to each ethnographic situation. I do not myself find much that is generally interesting in what social anthropologists have written about economic systems and in this book I have left the whole of that basic dimension on one side. I have already said a great deal about how I view the study of kinship. But what can one usefully say, in just a few pages, about the study of cosmologies?

The first point perhaps is that cosmologies are unconstrained. They are the creation of the human imagination; they do not have to conform to the inconvenient limitations of the real world. But secondly, because cosmologies are invented by human beings, they consist of transformations of the real-life experience of those who invent them. It follows that, at a structural (transformational) level, it is always quite certain that the patterns discernible in the cosmology – in the construction of the 'other world' and in the relationships between the 'other world' of the imagination and the 'this world' of lived experience – will also occur, in more mundane form, in the here and now, in full view of the anthropological observer. But thirdly, the 'other world' is close at hand.

Both these last points are difficult to demonstrate in a convincing manner. The traditional (religious) cosmology of Western civilization has become frozen by its literary form into a pattern which is wholly anachronistic. A deity who is

'King of kings, the only ruler of princes' made sense in the days of the Emperor Constantine and even in the England of the sixteenth century; but in a world cluttered with formulae about the equality of man and with institutions such as the United Nations Assembly, the imagery of God as Supreme Emperor has no place at all. Alternatively, the modern (scientific) cosmology of the astrophysicists, with its fables of the beginning of time in a Big Bang and a universe filled with inconceivable numbers of entities spaced at inconceivable distances of time and space, leads us to think that the cosmos is, in all respects, vast, so that 'the other world', if there were such a place, would certainly be a very long way away.

But the cosmologies encountered by anthropologists in the field are of quite a different kind. It was Vico who observed that, for the Greeks, the Underworld was no more distant than the bottom of a plough furrow, while the abode of the gods on Mount Olympus was at the top of a visible mountain of quite moderate size. In the course of my Kachin fieldwork I was told of a procedure whereby a spirit medium, in a state of trance, would ascend a ladder into the sky to consult personally with the sky deities (*mu nat*); the rungs of the ladder were sword blades with the sharp edge upwards. When I came to witness the actual performance of this seemingly miraculous event I found it something of an anti-climax. The medium ascended on to a platform about twenty feet above the ground and, although the rungs of the ladder did include one upturned sword blade, I noticed that the medium took good care not to step on it!

At the time I took this to be symbolical play-acting, but in retrospect, I feel that that was a wrong interpretation. A platform twenty feet above the ground in free air was indeed 'in the sky'; the 'other world' of the gods was as close as that.

So let me try to make my point by elaborating further a thumbnail sketch of traditional Kachin cosmology.

Kachin political ideology represents sky (*mu*) and earth (*ga*) as a binary pair, inseparable but opposed. When a Kachin lineage head referred to the territory of his lineage he would say 'our sky and earth' (*anhte a lamu ga*) not just 'our land'. In the Kachin creation story we start with male/female essences which, in the imagery of a primeval mist (male) copulating with a primeval bird (female), give birth to various non-human things and animals. Several episodes later we arrive at another combination of male/female essences, Chyanun(female) – Woishun(male). This androgynous being is the first ancestor of both the gods (*nat*) and of men.

There is great variety in the functions of the spiritual beings which the Kachin rate as *nat* but it is a mistake to suppose they can be sorted out as gods and demons on a good/bad basis. However, generally speaking, there is a distinction between nats which are 'magnified non-natural men' (to use Andrew Lang's phrase), who are potentially benevolent and who are regarded as either direct ancestors or *mayu ni* ('wife-givers to') direct ancestors, and nats which are magnified non-natural animals (i.e. monsters), most of whom are malevolent.

The *mayu ni* deity nats are superior to the direct-ancestor household nats just as, in real life, *mayu ni* who are of different political status to their *dama ni* will always be their superiors, but they fall into two categories, the sky nats (*mu*) and the river monsters (*baren*) (described in the literature as 'alligators'). The *baren* do not, so far as I know, receive any positive ritual attention but there is a suggestion that if it were not for their animal presence in our human ancestry we should all be gods rather than men; the *baren* are the source of our imperfections; roughly speaking, they play the role of the Serpent in our Adam and Eve story. A schematic arrangement of this mythological ancestry is shown in

Figure 7.1. (In the usual anthropological convention males are shown as triangles, females as circles.)

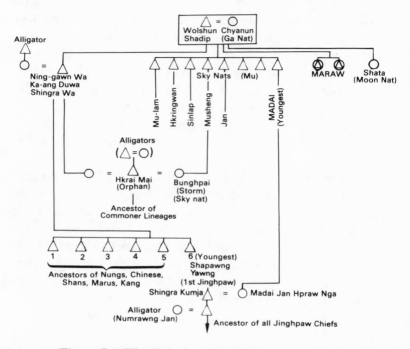

Figure 7.1: The Relationship of Humans to Gods

A point of importance here is that succession among the Kachin follows the principle of ultimogeniture; it is the youngest son who inherits the chiefly title as head of the lineage. So naturally it is the youngest of the sky nats, Madat, who is the prince among the sky nats, and who stands in a *mayu* relationship to the Kachin chiefs through his having given his daughter, Madai Jan Hpraw Nga, as wife to Shingra Kumja, the son of the first human ancestor of the Kachin.

But at this point look back at Figure 6.1 on p. 205. In that diagram, which represents the lay-out of a chief's house, the principal shrine is to the Madai Nat (7). It is located in my zone A/B, at house floor level, three feet or so above the stable area (1), which houses the sacrificial cattle (*nga*). The name 'Madai Jan Hpraw Nga' means 'Madai Lady White Cow'. In a complicated metaphorical way every chiefly sacrifice of an animal to the Madai Nat is a reaffirmation of this 'original' marriage link. The real world counterpart of the Madai Nat shrine (7) is the ladder of the new bride (4) which is adjacent to it (p. 207).

Here is the other half, as it were, of the same story. Men are not gods because their first semi-divine ancestor Ning-gawn Wa (Ka-ang Duwa, top left of Figure 7.1) married a *baren*. When the *baren* girl was brought from her river home to Ning-gawn Wa's palace she stank (i.e., 'was polluted'); no amount of washing would remove the smell. The eventual solution to this problem was to put her through a purification ritual in which she walked through an avenue of 'bundles of thatching grass planted in the ground before the house'. Present-day brides, immediately before they enter their new home and ascend the new porch ladder, must walk through just such an avenue. To each bunch of grass is attached a live pig which is killed as the bride passes by so that the blood spurts out on to her feet. There would normally be six bunches of grass and six pigs. The principal pig is provided by the bride's party. The six are in three sets of two and constitute sacrifices to the household ancestor spirits (*nat tawn*) and to the household 'luck' spirits (*maraw*) of the households of (a) the bride's father, (b) the intermediary who arranged the terms of the marriage, and (c) the groom's father, in that order.

Prior to this, the bride has first set out in ceremonial procession from her own home, moving first to the house of the intermediary and then to a matted space twenty yards or so from the front of her father-in-law's house. The procession includes both males and females but, for once in her life, the bride does not carry a basket on her back. Two baskets containing various specified symbolic objects, which are a kind of bride's trousseau, are carried in the procession by two unmarried girls who should not be her immediate sisters. The parents are never present but the party should include an elderly female chaperon who should be, in the ideal case, a father's sister (*moi*).

Before the bride goes through her blood bespattered rite of aggregation into her new home, there are many preliminaries. The six bunches of grass have to be sanctified by sacrifices performed by three different priests appointed by the heads of the three households concerned, and there is a counter procession of young men from the groom's household with much drum-beating and dancing, by the end of which the bride and her immediate attendants are seated on newly made stools on the matted space aforesaid. They may sit there for a long time for at this point, in honour of the bride, it is the duty of the intermediary to try to negotiate an increase in the bridewealth payment and the proceedings may become highly acrimonious.[1]

The mat-sitting phase of the ceremony is, in Van Gennep's language, the *rite de marge* (cf. p. 202); the pig slaughter and the mounting of the new ladder are the 'rite of aggregation'. Note that the purification element in the ritual matches that in phase 17 of my Sinhalese wedding story (p. 197). The point about the father's sister (*moi*) of the bride is that this lady has the kinship status of a relative who is already married into the *dama* lineage which the bride is about to enter. The *moi* holds the bride's hand as she walks through the avenue of slaughtered pigs and up the new ladder. This detail emphasizes the 'aggregation' aspect of the procedure.

Here are some further 'cosmological' points which have general rather than particular interest.

The never-never land where the first human beings lived is usually described as Majoi Shingra Bum, a literal gloss of which is 'the mountain that is everywhere flat'. This nice contradiction in terms was interpreted by the early missionaries as meaning that the Kachin had a tradition that they had come from the Tibetan Plateau, and elaborate theories of ethnic migrations have been built on this foundation. The 'ethnologists' concerned failed to notice that the chief of this mysterious country is called the Ka-ang Duwa, 'the Prince of the Centre of the Earth'. Both terms simply serve to emphasize that this country is in the 'other' world, not this one.

The boundary between 'this world', the land of the living, and the 'other world', the land of the dead, is always marked by ambiguity. In Christian legend Saint Peter holds the keys of heaven but his biblical status is very equivocal and in medieval tradition the stories about Simon Peter ('Simon the Rock') were all mixed up with stories about Simon Magus ('Simon the corruptible magician'). Ganesha, the guardian of thresholds in Hindu story, is incorruptible but he is also highly ambiguous; part-man/part-elephant in form; part-yogi/part-demon in function. This pattern is very common and there is a whole literature about the trickster figures who bar the way to Paradise. In Kachin legend this role is filled by the chameleon; a small creature but one which possesses the capacity to adjust its colouring very rapidly to its surroundings!

Finally to go back to sky and earth as a binary pair. Look again at Figure 6.1 on p. 205. The animals are on ground level; the human beings and the nat shrines are above ground level. And, if I am right in thinking that the sky may start at a height of twenty feet or so, then the human beings are halfway between heaven and earth, part-god, part-animal, which is just what we have been saying all along.

That seems to be a sensible place to stop. Taken by itself mythology appears as pure fantasy but if one considers myth in context and notes how even quite trivial details in the 'way of life' of the people who use it are ratified in the details of the myth itself, we begin to see that what is being 'said', both by the myth as text and by the actors in performance, is something altogether different from the childish superstition with which 'savages' were credited by the anthropologists of Frazer's generation. There is no possibility of developing this thesis in detail in the space available to me but perhaps my skeletal account of certain features of the muddling mass of Kachin ethnography will give you some idea of what I mean.

Conclusion

And that really is all I am going to say. I have grandly entitled my book *Social Anthropology* but not only does it contain a good deal that has very little to do with social anthropology, as ordinarily understood, but there are huge areas of contemporary social anthropological practice which are completely ignored. To take just one such area, I have said nothing at all about the study of witchcraft which is a field to which social anthropologists have made very positive and enlightening contributions.

Yet what I might have said about witchcraft-theory would only have been the converse of what I have written about legitimacy. Legitimate relations are those in which the direction of power flow is compatible with the interests of those who exercise authority in the social system as it is now. Such relationships are modelled on ideas about benevolent interaction between supernatural powers and men; in witchcraft relations just the reverse is the case. The power of the witch is seen as a threat to the established order.

For example, in the Kachin case, where spirit mediums (*myihtoi*-'seers of light') were possessed by and conversed with benevolent spiritual beings who were ancestors, witches (*hpyi*) were possessed by and conversed with malevolent spiritual beings who were not ancestors. Witchcraft was associated with improper food and improper sex relations.

Where the paradigm of relations between gods and men

was provided by the *mayu/dama* pattern – wife-givers dominant over wife-receivers – the paradigm of witchcraft was provided by 'incest' (*jaiwawng*) in which sex relations between a *mayu* boy and a *dama* girl produced a monstrous child. The paradox here was that, since it was taken for granted that all unmarried girls engaged in 'incestuous' relationships of this sort, all unmarried girls were potential witches! But that is a complication which I cannot here pursue.

Instead of trying to cover the total field, or even a substantial part of the total field, I have proceeded along the course briefly plotted out in my Introduction. I have concerned myself with various kinds of discontinuous binary oppositions of the $+/-$ sort and with the complementary fact that such distinctions, although they are quite fundamental to the manner in which human beings manage to persuade themselves that social life is orderly, are imposed on a background of real-life experience which is continuous both in time and in space. It is only at this abstract level that different social systems become comparable. They represent alternative solutions to problems of intellectual paradox.

The book as a whole has proceeded from the extremes of generality to the extremes of particularity, from man as a cosmic being to the minutiae of Kachin ethnography. The practising anthropologist handles matters just the other way round. He first encounters the minutiae of ethnography and then reflects upon how far such details may perhaps be relevant for our understanding of man as a cosmic being. I have endeavoured all the way through the book to exhibit these two facets of the anthropologist's endeavour and to show how intimately they are interconnected.

Critics of this style of anthropology tend to say that it does not 'explain' anything. It does not provide an account of how things originated. That is true, but, for my part, I am not greatly interested in 'origins'. It would of course be nice to know how things came to be as they are, but making guesses about such matters is not 'explanation'.

The form of a particular social system is not 'determined' by the manner of its adaptation to the environmental ecosystem in the way some vulgar Marxists, sociobiologists, and cultural materialists seem to believe, though the past history of a society's cultural experience clearly sets limits upon what is at all probable. Yet, as the vulgar Marxists have long argued, the infrastructure of economic necessity and the superstructure of the ideology of legitimate authority do form one of the crucial 'binary oppositions' that every social anthropologist has to unravel.

In the field, as the social anthropologist experiences it, the incongruities and discontinuities between 'economic facts' and 'ideological theories' are given an appearance of congruence and continuity by the way in which what I have called 'the dimension of kinship' is made to permeate both the organization of labour and the relations between physical man and the metaphysical other.

The thesis that runs right through this book is that it is only when we come to understand that relationships between man and man and man and god are, at least in a metaphorical sense, the equivalent of economic indebtedness, that we can really appreciate how this transformation of economics into ideology through the mediation of kinship actually occurs. So it is really Chapter 5, which elaborates a sociological theory of debt, which provides the keystone to my argument.

I am aware that the essentially functionalist style of my presentation, in which everything seems to fit together with everything else, may suggest that I believe, like the founders of social anthropology fifty years ago, that everything is for the best in the best of all possible worlds, and that the 'savage' societies which social anthropologists like to study have an inherent stability rather than, as the Marxists would maintain, an inherent instability.

In fact I believe nothing of the sort. On the contrary, almost all societies which have ever been encountered by literary man were undergoing change, sometimes very drastic change, before literary man encountered them. And the arrival of the foreigners with their new commodities invariably greatly speeded up the process.

But to say that social change is always occurring is one thing; to say that we 'understand' the nature of such change or that we can somehow predict what sort of changes will occur in the future is quite another. I do not think that social anthropology in its present form has much to contribute to the study of the dynamics of social systems. But that does not worry me overmuch.

Let me remind you that I started out as an engineer. In the elementary theory of engineering constructions, I learned first about 'statics' and later about 'dynamics', but it then turned out that all the really basic theory was in the 'statics' volume and that 'dynamics' was a kind of supplementary gloss upon what I had learned already.

Social anthropology is, I agree, the study of the statics of social systems. I also agree that, in the real world, social systems are never in a state of stasis and very seldom even in a state of dynamic equilibrium. But a proper understanding of such an 'as if', unreal, theory of social statics can still be of genuine value. Anyway, for the past forty years, I personally have found it absorbingly interesting.

Glossary

I had optimistically imagined that I had managed to write this book without resort to jargon but when the editor pointed out that a reader who encounters such an expression as 'synchronic functional interdependence between institutions' (p. 27) would be unlikely to share that view, I had to think again. Actually, I have explained a number of technical terms in the body of the text and it is difficult to know where jargon begins and ends. 'Nomothetic' and 'sibling' are both ordinary dictionary words (provided you have the right dictionary!) but some readers who would recoil from the former might feel insulted to be told the meaning of the latter and other readers might never have encountered either.

So the selection of glosses is very arbitrary. I have gone through my text with a red pencil marking words and phrases that look awkward and then added a small scatter of fairly unfamiliar terms which I may not have used at all but which are certainly part of the common language of social anthropology. The list is old-fashioned. All the terms it contains have been around for at least thirty years. I have not included any of the current jargon favoured by Marxist anthropologists nor any of the constantly proliferating neologisms of American cultural anthropology. The list includes a few words which were originally used by anthropologists as technical jargon, e.g.: exogamy, endogamy, taboo, which have by now become part of the ordinary vernacular language. I have included them here just to remind the reader that in the writings of anthropologists these still remain technical terms rather than common language terms, a circumstance which sometimes leads to misunderstanding.

1 *Acephalous*: lit. 'headless'. 'Acephalous societies' are social systems which operate cohesively as political entities without there being any centralized state organization. It has been used by Africanist anthropologists to describe a wide range of societies including the Nuer (Southern Sudan) and the Tallensi (Northern Ghana).

2 *Affinity*: relationship resulting from 'marriage' rather than from descent from a common ancestor. Contrasted with 'consanguinity' (see below). Many social anthropologists take it for granted that 'affinal relationships' form a distinct category in all human societies. This entails the supposition that 'marriage' is a universal human institution, a proposition which begs many basic questions. Followers of Lévi-Strauss use the term 'alliance' to denote the bonding of social groups through a tie (or ties) of affinity in contrast to the bond which links together segments of a single lineage through common descent.

3 *Alliance*: see 'affinity'.

4 *Animism*: the term used by E. B. Tylor to denote what he regarded as the typical form of 'primitive religion' which was said to involve a belief that non-human material objects, plants and animals, possess 'souls'. Tylor's animism is not easily distinguished from what other nineteenth-century anthropologists described as 'fetishism'.

5 *Bilateral kinship*: contrasted with unilineal descent. In the absence of any kind of mating between cousins, second cousins, etc., each individual has two parents, four grandparents, eight great-grandparents . . . and is related by 'bilateral kinship' to all individuals descended through either

male or female links from all such ancestors. 'Kinship', in this comprehensive ramifying sense, has biological significance but is of limited social importance because it fails to segment humanity into distinguishable groups; ultimately, whoever you are, my kin and your kin are the same . . . we are all descended from Adam! In societies which operate a system of 'unilineal descent' (see 'descent') the individual's parents almost invariably belong to different 'unilineal descent groups' (lineages). The individual will ordinarily have ties of kinship with both these groups, but they are ties of quite different kinds. Some anthropologists make a distinction between kinship in this sense, which depends upon links of 'filiation' (q.v.), and ties of 'affinity' (q.v.). In this usage (which is not my own) authors usually write of 'kinship and marriage', implying that 'affinal relationships' are not 'kinship'.

6 *Brideprice(bridewealth)*: in most human societies the institution which social anthropologists label 'marriage' is a contractual arrangement between two groups of kinsmen rather than a simple pairing off of a man and a woman. The marriage creates (or reaffirms) a bond of affinity (alliance) between the two groups. The transfer of rights over the woman (and her potential offspring) from her natal group to her husband's group initiates a chain of reciprocities – expressed in the transfer of goods and services of various kinds – which may continue for years, perhaps for generations. The principal payments from the husband and his kin to the kin of the bride are commonly referred to as 'brideprice' (or 'bridewealth'). Such payments are not a 'price' in any simple sense – the bride is not 'sold' – but the transactions in question can be of great economic importance (see also 'dowry').

7. *Charisma*: 'divine grace'. A concept originally introduced into sociology by Max Weber where the 'charismatic authority' of inspired prophets is contrasted with the

'legitimate authority' of office holders. The point about 'charismatic authority' is that it is not delegated from others. However, in the last analysis, all authority is charismatic since at the top of any hierarchy of office holders there is an office which is deemed to be potent in itself. Thus Weber eventually came to write of the 'charisma' attaching to high offices, e.g. that of the Emperor of China.

8 *Classificatory kinship terminologies*: most contemporary inhabitants of the British Isles have a very limited range of recognized kin and they use kinship terms such as brother, sister, father, mother, uncle, aunt in a very restricted way. In many human societies most of the words denoting such relationships are non-specific category terms which include large numbers of individuals, rather as an English speaker might say: 'Oh, he is a cousin of some sort.' Readers of anthropological monographs need to remember this. Reference to a 'mother's brother's daughter' has to be understood in the light of the fact that every individual may address a number of different women as 'mother', a number of 'parallel cousins' (see 'cousins') as 'brother', and a number of fairly remote 'nieces' as 'daughter'.

9 *Consanguinity*: lit. 'of the same blood', contrasted with 'affinity' (q.v.). This term is now seldom used by anthropologists but Morgan's classic study of kinship terminologies, published in 1871, was called *Systems of Consanguinity and Affinity of the Human Family*. This distinguishes 'consanguinity' from 'affinity' in approximately the same way as some recent authors have distinguished 'kinship' from 'marriage' (see 'bilateral kinship' above).

10 *Cosmology*: when modern theoretical astronomers refer to 'cosmology' they mean a theory about the origin of the universe and its present total structure. Although such theories are regarded as 'scientific' in the purest Royal Society sense they change with great rapidity and ultimately

rest upon a substantial body of unverified (and perhaps unverifiable) beliefs. The systems of beliefs and practices which social anthropologists commonly refer to as 'primitive religion' are concerned with cosmologies in this sense and in this book 'cosmology' has this meaning (see also 'religion').

11 *Cousins*: (a) *cross-cousin* – the relationship between two individuals where the mother of the one is sister to the father of the other; (b) *parallel cousin* – the relationship between two individuals where *either* the two mothers *or* the two fathers are siblings to one another.

In many societies the cross-cousin relationship is sharply contrasted with the parallel cousin relationship. (See also 'patrilateral/matrilateral'.)

12 *Descent*: contrasted with 'filiation' (q.v.). Different anthropologists use this important term in several slightly different ways. In general, British usage is more precise than that of either the Americans or the French but is not uniform. I myself here follow Fortes who holds that 'descent' is only meaningful in a context of unilineal descent groups (lineages). The members of a single lineage share their sense of common identity by virtue of a claim that they are all descended through links of one sex (either all male [patrilineal descent] or all female [matrilineal descent]) from a common ancestor. The terms 'patrilineage' and 'matri-lineage' denote patrilineal and matrilineal lineages respectively.

13 *Divination*: a term covering a very wide range of techniques (including those of consulting oracles and casting horoscopes) which purport to foretell the future and thereby provide a basis for action by the individual who is consulting the diviner. While some of the forms of divination practised in exotic cultures will strike the reader as highly bizarre, it should be remembered that our own social system gives employment to a wide range of diviners – economists,

meteorologists, opinion pollsters, psychiatrists etc. – whose demonstrated capacity for accurate prediction is no better and no worse than that of, say, the operators of the Azande poison oracle. (See also 'shamanism'.)

14 *Dowry*: the property endowment which a bride brings with her into her husband's domestic household at the time of marriage. Not to be confused with a reversed 'brideprice' ('bridegroom price'). In legal theory a woman's 'dowry' is her personal property and not the property of her husband.

15 *Endogamy*: a rule which specifies that in legally recognized marriage the husband and the wife must be members of the same social group as specified by the rule, e.g. in orthodox Judaism a Jewish man must always marry a Jewish woman and vice versa.

16 *Exogamy*: a rule which specifies that in legally recognized marriage the husband and the wife must come from different social groups as specified by the rule, e.g. in European society one such normal rule is that a man and a woman cannot marry if they share a common parent. In systems of unilineal descent (see 'descent') it is usually the case that lineages of small scale are exogamous. Some anthropologists write as if 'exogamy' were the direct converse of 'incest'. But this is over simple. Incest rules relate to sexual intercourse; exogamy rules are concerned with legal contracts of 'marriage'.

17 *Filiation*: contrasted with 'descent' (q.v.). The immediate one-generation bond between a child and either of its parents. In Fortes' usage the term 'complementary filiation' denotes the filiation link with the parent who is *not* of the same descent group as the child: e.g. in a patrilineal system complementary filiation denotes the link of filiation between a child and its mother.

18 *Fitness* (Darwinian): I have twice used the expression 'the Darwinian dogma of the *survival of the fittest*'. Purists may object. The phrase was, I believe, coined by Herbert Spencer who thought of evolution as a process resulting from ruthless competition for scarce resources; surviving species were the 'winners' in such competition. In Darwinian theory, on the other hand, 'fitness' refers to 'goodness of fit'. Species, considered as collectivities of individuals, are always undergoing random variation as a result of mutations. Occasionally such a mutation will produce an organism which is able to make use of previously unused resources in the local biological/ecologist system and which on that account is more likely to transmit its characteristics to succeeding generations than other less well-adapted individuals. On this theory species 'survive' by finding (by chance) an ecological niche where they are *not* in direct competition with other organisms. Because of rapid advances in genetics Darwinian-type theories are currently undergoing drastic modification.

Theorizing about the processes of social evolution has a much longer history than theorizing about the processes of biological evolution. There is no obvious reason to suppose that any close analogy can be drawn between the two types of historical process. Social change is a very rapid process; biological evolution is always slow and usually very slow. The kinds of change which some authors consider to be symptoms of 'social evolution' are 'Lamarckian' rather than 'Darwinian' in that they manifestly depend upon the 'inheritance of acquired characteristics' from one generation to the next.

19 *Functionalism*: various aspects of various forms of anthropological functionalism are discussed in my text. The distinguishing characteristic of functionalist anthropologists is the value which they attach to understanding how social institutions, which can be observed to co-exist at a given time in a given place, 'fit together' to make a more or less coherent

whole which 'makes sense' to the participant actors. Functionalism, in this sense, contrasts with various types of anthropology in which the investigator dissects a system of social institutions into its component parts and then makes cross-cultural comparisons of the separate components; e.g. studies in which mythologies or kinship terminologies are discussed and compared without reference to the details of the social context in which they were originally embedded are fundamentally 'anti-functionalist'.

20 *Functionalist empiricism*: contrasted in my text with *structuralist idealism* (or sometimes *structuralist rationalism*). What we feel we know about the world out there derives from the interpretations which we put upon our sense perceptions. These interpretations are clearly greatly influenced by our education and the way we use language. The data of anthropology thus consist on the one hand of things and observed behaviours 'out there in the world' and on the other hand of ideas, symbols, beliefs, values etc. 'in people's heads'. The anthropologists whom I have labelled 'functionalist empiricists' (e.g. Malinowski, Firth) are behaviourists. They are prepared to trust their senses and concern themselves primarily with supposedly 'objective facts' out there in the world. By contrast, the anthropologists who are of 'structuralist idealist' persuasion (e.g. Lévi-Strauss, Schneider) distrust their sense perceptions and concentrate their interest on the patterning of ideas as revealed through symbolism and linguistic usages. Nearly all contemporary social anthropologists are cultural relativists to some degree – they are sceptical of the notion that there are universal 'natural laws' from which a rational morality might be derived – but the functionalist empiricists are much less extreme in their commitment to cultural relativity than some of their colleagues.

21 *Genitor* (from the Latin): the biological male parent of a child. Some societies make a clear distinction between the

status of the *genitor* as such and that of the *pater* – the legal father – whose status has been established through a 'marriage contract' with the child's mother. The *genitor* and the *pater* are in most cases the same individual but there are many societies in which the status of *pater* may be allocated to a woman. It is sometimes necessary to draw further distinctions, e.g. between the actual biological *genitor* and the publicly acknowledged *genitor*; it is sometimes possible for the roles of the *pater* to be subdivided between more than one 'male' parent.

22 *Homeostatic equilibrium*: in Durkheimian sociology and the structural-functional anthropology which derived from it it was often assumed that in a 'healthy' condition a society will always be in stable (i.e. homeostatic) equilibrium in the sense that if the 'natural' organic integration of the system is disturbed social forces will come into play which will quickly bring things back to 'normality'. Societies where this homeostatic recovery process failed to operate were considered to be in a pathological condition. References to 'equilibrium' in anthropological literature always seem to refer to stable equilibrium. Unstable equilibrium (e.g. that of an egg balanced on its sharp end) is never considered. Contemporary social anthropologists are much less committed to the belief that the facts under observation form part of an integrated stable social system.

23 *HRAF*: 'Human Relations Area Files'. An elaborate system for the abstracting and filing of the ethnographic contents of anthropological monographs initiated by G. P. Murdock when he was Professor of Anthropology at Yale but now operated independently. There is a wide divergence of view among professional anthropologists as to whether or not the indexing of ethnographic materials in this form serves any useful purpose.

24 *Incest*: all societies have sets of moral evaluations which

purport to regulate sexual behaviour. Some of the resultant prohibitions are commonly referred to as 'incest taboos'. Much of the resulting anthropological literature is thoroughly unsatisfactory, first because it presupposes that there is something universal about the particular set of prohibitions which are categorized as 'incest' in the English language or in English law and secondly because 'incest' (sexual intercourse between particular pairs of closely related kin) tends to be discussed in isolation from other sexual 'offences' such as 'adultery', 'bestiality', 'homo-sexuality'.

25 *Institution*: this term appears very frequently in the writings of social anthropologists but is very loosely used. My own usage is close to that of Malinowski. Here the concept 'institution' embraces not only a particular set of customary arrangements but also the personnel who are involved in those arrangements, the resources and technical know-how which they employ in their performances, the 'rules of the game', and the 'mythical charter' which provides a justification for the existence of the institution and its perpetuation.

26 *Jural rules*: as distinct from *legal rules*. Rules which effect the rights and obligations of individuals and which have the force of law but which are sanctioned by custom rather than legislation.

27 *Kindred*: all the descendants through all links (male and female) from a common ancestor. A kindred, thus defined, does not constitute a discrete group of individuals (see 'bilateral kinship'). Where kindreds operate as effective social units they are delimited by some factor other than 'descent from a common ancestor', e.g. by the fact that all the members live in one locality or that they all have rights in a common estate.

28 *Lineage principle*: the principle by which social solidarity is based in a belief in unilineal descent from a common ancestor. (See also 'descent', 'segmentary lineages'.)

29 *Magic*: anthropological literature of the Frazerian era gives the impression that 'magic' is of central concern to anthropologists and that it is readily recognisable as 'non-rational purposive action'. Few contemporary social anthropologists would confidently assert that they can distinguish a magical from a non-magical act. Virtually all kinds of purposive actions contain elements which are not strictly 'necessary' from a mechanistic point of view but which have 'symbolic' value for the actor. The performances which are described as 'magic' in ethnographic literature are ones in which this symbolic component is very pronounced but they do not form a distinct class of actions. (See also 'sorcery'.)

30 *Marriage*: most anthropological monographs are written as if 'marriage' were a universal institution. In this book it is argued that while the various institutions that have been described as 'marriage' have a certain family resemblance they are not strictly comparable from a sociological point of view. (See Chapter 6.)

31 *Matrilineal*: opposite to *patrilineal*. (See 'descent'.)

32 *Nomothetic*: this unfamiliar word has a prominent place in the writings of both Radcliffe-Brown and Marvin Harris. It refers to a belief on the part of the authors concerned that the task of the anthropologist is to discover 'general laws' of social or cultural process on the model of the general laws enunciated in the natural sciences. No such general laws other than trivialities have yet been discovered.

33 *Pater*: see *genitor*.

34 *Patrilateral/matrilateral*: terms used to distinguish two types of cross-cousin (see 'cousins'). Patrilateral ('father's side') cross-cousins are the children of Ego's father's sisters; matrilateral ('mother's side') cross-cousins are the children of Ego's mother's brothers. Thus a system of matrilateral cross-cousin marriage is one in which, in every regular marriage, the husband and the wife are related as A/b, which is the same classificatory relationship as that which includes 'father's sister's son'/'mother's brother's daughter'.

35 *Patrilineal*: opposite to *matrilineal*. (See 'descent'.)

36 *Polysemic*: 'having several meanings'. It is characteristic of ritual performances everywhere that there are several 'layers of meaning' each of which is metaphoric of all the others. Inadequate appreciation of this fact was a major defect in earlier anthropological discussions of 'magical' performance.

37 *Religion*: in contemporary English vernacular the word 'religion' presupposes the existence of a church organization and professional clergymen. Since these features are usually absent from the 'primitive religions' described by social anthropologists it might be less misleading if they used a different term. In this book 'cosmology' (q.v.) is used as the equivalent of the anthropologists' 'primitive religion'.

38 *Segmentary lineages*: lineage systems (systems of unilineal descent) are commonly organized in a hierarchy, such that a maximum lineage A encompasses segments A1 and A2, which in turn encompass further segments A1.a, A1.b; A2.a, A2.b . . . and so on. There is a comparable hierarchy of feelings of 'solidarity' and 'opposition' ('we'/'they'). All members of A may unite in opposition to a comparable aggregate B; but in a different context all members of A1 may unite in opposition to A2 or all members of A1.a may unite in opposition to A2.b. This type of social structure,

which Durkheim labelled 'mechanical solidarity', is not peculiar to lineage systems but is characteristic of most such systems.

39 *Shamanism*: properly speaking applicable only to the specialized form of spirit medium cult found in Siberia. In recent literature 'shaman' may refer to a spirit medium of almost any kind, i.e. any form of cult activity in which the medium, in a state of trance, purports to speak in the capacity of a spiritual being from the other world. In this general sense shamanism is a world-wide phenomenon. From some points of view it may be considered a form of 'divination' (q.v.).

40 *Sibling*: the relationship linking any two children of the same parents including brother/brother, sister/sister, and brother/sister.

41 *Social structure*: this expression is used by social and cultural anthropologists in a variety of senses. British social anthropologists ordinarily follow Radcliffe-Brown. The society as a whole is envisaged as a kind of organism in which the various institutions (q.v.) are articulated together to form a functioning whole. The social structure is the persisting framework of such a self-perpetuating system. An approximate analogy is that the relationship between the social structure and the society as a whole is comparable to the relationship between the bony skeleton of a living mammal and its total bodily form. This use of the word 'structure' has very little in common with the 'social structure' of G. P. Murdock, which assumes that a society is an aggregate of separate entities like the bricks which go to make up a building, or the 'structure' of Lévi-Strauss, which is concerned with the abstract (mathematical) ordering of patterns rather than their concrete manifestations.

42 *Sorcery*: notionally the use of 'magic' for the purpose of

bringing misfortune to others. Nowadays anthropologists are more interested in the reputation of sorcerers and in the circumstances that lead to accusations of sorcery than in its actual performance. In some societies a distinction can be drawn between 'witchcraft', which entails a belief that the 'witch' has metaphysical powers (e.g., that the witch's disembodied spirit can remove its victim's entrails while the latter is asleep), and sorcery, which is viewed as a strictly mechanical process. But with witchcraft, as with sorcery, the anthropologist is usually more interested in the social relationships which link accuser to accused and accused to alleged victim than with the details of what is supposed to happen. (See also 'divination'.)

43 *Structural-functionalism*: a latter-day expression used to distinguish the functionalism of the followers of Radcliffe-Brown from the functionalism of Malinowski. (See 'functionalism'.) Structural-functionalism is essentially the functionalism that was spelled out by Durkheim in *The Division of Labour* (1893) blended with the 'ideal type' sociology of Max Weber. In this schema the function of an institution is the part which it plays in maintaining the viability of the society as a whole – the model analogy being that 'the function of a mammalian heart is to ensure the circulation of the blood'. In the contrasted Malinowskian view the function of an institution is its contribution to the likelihood that individual members of the society will survive. (See also 'social structure'.)

44 *Structuralism*: as used in this book the term 'structuralism' refers to the distinctive style of anthropological practice developed by Lévi-Strauss from 1945 onwards. The basic idea is that cultural forms are interesting because of the patterns which they contain which, in various transformations, represent expressions of very basic configurations of human thought. The ultimate objective of the anthropologist, on this view, is not the understanding of particular

social systems but the decoding of the principles through which the human mind operates.

45 *Structural idealism*: see 'functionalist empiricism'.

46 *Synchronic/diachronic*: the contrast between viewing a social system all at one moment of time, as in a photograph, and viewing the same system as a sequence of historical events. The studies of social anthropologists are mostly synchronic analyses; they tend to represent particular societies as 'more or less' functionally integrated at a particular point in time. Social anthropologists justify analyses of this sort by arguing that if you do not possess historical evidence of what actually happened in the past it is a waste of time to invent it.

47 *Taboo*: the word is of Polynesian/Melanesian origin but in modern anthropology it has become a technical term. An action or object or space is said to be 'taboo' if it is 'forbidden' to perform it, touch it, eat it, enter it, etc. There can be many rationalizations for such prohibition: breach of the taboo would be 'dangerous', 'disgusting', 'sacrilegious', 'contrary to custom'. An impressive body of anthropological theory is centrally concerned with why the foci of taboo fall where they do. This theory bears directly on the main theme of this book which concerns the relationship between continuity and discontinuity in human affairs.

48 *Totemism*: 'the worship of animals and plants'. During the late-nineteenth century 'totemism' was the principal rival to Tylor's 'animism' (q.v.) as the characteristic form of 'primitive religion'.

49 *Witchcraft*: see 'sorcery'.

Notes

Introduction

1. See, e.g., the diagram at p. 49 of Lévi-Strauss (1968), first published in 1945.

1 The Diversity of Anthropology

1. Engels (1884) is a kind of Marxist gloss on Morgan (1877).
2. Source: letter by Haddon in author's possession.
3. Evans-Pritchard (1935), p. 186.
4. Lévi-Strauss' book of this title carries the English title *The Savage Mind* which is wholly misleading.
5. This appears to be the general argument of Wilson (1978) though the author contradicts himself so frequently that he might easily protest that his thesis is something quite different. Some of Wilson's disciples have spelled out the argument much more explicitly; see Dawkins (1979).
6. Tylor (1871), pp. 1, 7, 12.
7. Harris (1978), esp. Chapter 9.
8. Schneider (1976).
9. Tylor (1889).
10. Harris (1979), p. 47.
11. Geertz and Geertz (1975), p. 2.
12. Source: Professor Jack Golson, Australian National University.
13. Hopkins (1980).
14. Evans-Pritchard (1965), p. 12.

2 The Unity of Man

1. de Maistre (1797).
2. Hodgen (1964), p. 112.
3. Montaigne [1958], Book 1, Chapter 31.
4. Petty Papers, II, 30–31, quoted in Hodgen (1964), pp. 421–2.
5. Mandeville, Prologue.
6. Tyson (1708).
7. Vico (1744).
8. Locke (1690), Book 1, Chapter 3, para. 9.
9. Gramsci [1957], p. 140.
10. Source: unpublished lecture by C. R. Boxer.

3 Humanity and Animality

1. Genesis, Chapter 3, v. 21.
2. More (1653), pp. 236–7.
3. The issue deserves serious consideration; St Guinefort was a dog. See Schmitt (1979).
4. Buettner-Janusch (1966), p. 347.
5. See Sebeok and Sebeok (eds) (1980).

4 My Kind of Anthropology

1. Hsu (1949), p. ix.
2. The phrase or something very like it originated with Bertrand de Jouvenel but I cannot now locate it.
3. Hugh-Jones, C. (1979), pp. 1, 13.

5 Debt, Relationship, Power

1. Turner (1969).
2. Maine (1861) (at p. 170 of the 9th edition [1883]).
3. De Tocqueville, *Democracy in America*, as quoted by Dumont (1966) (at p. 18 of the 1970 edition).

6 Marriage, Legitimacy, Alliance

1. This formula appears in the 1951 edition of *Notes and Queries in Anthropology*. It seems to have originated with Radcliffe-Brown.
2. See especially Evans-Pritchard (1940), (1951), (1956).
3. See especially Gough (1961) and connected references.
4. Van Gennep (1908); Hertz (1907).
5. Cline (1936).

7 Some Aspects of Cosmology

1. The account of Kachin marriage ceremonial given in Chapter 15 of Hanson (1913) is both detailed and trustworthy.

Bibliography

Arens, W. (1979), *The Man-Eating Myth: Anthropology and Anthropophagy* (New York: Oxford University Press)

Buettner-Janusch, J. (1966), *Origins of Man: Physical Anthropology* (New York: Wiley)

Cline, W. (1936), *Notes on the People of Siwah and el-Garah in the Libyan Desert* (Menasha: George Banta Publishing Co.)

D'Oyly, J. (1929), *A Sketch of the Constitution of the Kandyan Kingdom* (Colombo: Government Printer)

Darwin, C. (1872), *The Expression of the Emotions in Man and Animals* (London: Murray)

Dawkins, R. (1979), *The Selfish Gene* (New York: Oxford University Press)

Dumont, L. (1970), *Homo Hierarchicus: The Caste System and its Implications* (London: Weidenfeld and Nicolson)

Durkheim, E. (1893), *De la division du travail social* (Paris: Alcan)

Engels, F. (1884), *The Origin of the Family, Private Property and the State* (English translation 1940, London: Lawrence and Wishart)

Evans-Pritchard, E. E. (1935), 'Science and Sentiment: an exposition and criticism of the writings of Pareto', *Bulletin of the Faculty of Arts; University of Egypt*, Vol. 3, Part 2, (December 1935 [Giza])

—— (1940), *The Nuer* (Oxford: Clarendon Press)

—— (1951), *Kinship and Marriage among the Nuer* (Oxford: Clarendon Press)

—— (1956), *Nuer Religion* (Oxford: Clarendon Press)

—— (1965), *Theories of Primitive Religion* (Oxford: Clarendon Press)

Fei, Hsiao-Tung (1939), *Peasant Life in China* (London: Routledge)

Firth, R. (1936), *We, The Tikopia: A Sociological Study of Kinship in Primitive Polynesia* (London: Allen and Unwin)

—— (1959), *Social Change in Tikopia: Re-Study of a Polynesian Community after a Generation* (London: Allen and Unwin)

Fitzgerald, C. P. (1941), *The Tower of Five Glories: A Study of the Min Chia of Ta Li, Yunnan* (London: Cresset Press)

Fortes, M. (1945), *The Dynamics of Clanship among the Tellensi* (London: Oxford University Press)

—— (1949), *The Web of Kinship among the Tallensi* (London: Oxford University Press)

Fortes, M. and Evans-Pritchard E. E. (1940), *African Political Systems* (London: Oxford University Press)

Foucault, M. (1966), *Les Mots et Les Choses* (Paris: Gallimard)

Frazer, J. G. (1890) *The Golden Bough* (London: Macmillan [various editions])

Geertz, H. and Geertz, C. (1975), *Kinship in Bali* (Chicago: University of Chicago Press)

Goody, J. (1976), *Production and Reproduction: A Comparative Study in the Domestic Domain* (Cambridge: Cambridge University Press)

Gough, K. (1961), Chapters 6, 7, 8 of D. M. Schneider and Kathleen Gough (Eds) *Matrilineal Kinship* (Berkeley: University of California Press)

Gramsci, A. (1957), *The Modern Prince and Other Writings* (translated by Louis Marks, New York: International Publishers)

Hanson, O. (1913), *The Kachins: their Customs and Traditions* (Rangoon: American Baptist Mission Press)

Harris, M. (1969), *The Rise of Anthropological Theory: A History of Theories of Culture* (London: Routledge and Kegan Paul)

—— (1978), *Cannibals and Kings: The Origins of Cultures* (London: Collins)

—— (1979), *Cultural Materialism: The Struggle for a Science of Culture* (New York: Random House)

Hertz, R. (1907), 'Contribution à une étude sur la représentation collective de la mort', *Année Sociologique*, Vol X (1907), pp. 48–137.

Hobbes, T. (1651), *Leviathan* (London)

Hodgen, M. T. (1964), *Early Anthropology in the Sixteenth and Seventeenth Centuries* (Philadelphia: Philadelphia University Press)

Hopkins, K. (1980), 'Brother-Sister Marriage in Roman Egypt' in *Comparative Studies in Society and History*, vol. 22, pp. 303–54.

Hsu, F. L. K. (1949), *Under the Ancestors' Shadow: Chinese Culture and Personality* (London: Routledge and Kegan Paul)

Hugh-Jones, C. (1979), *From the Milk River: Spatial and Temporal Processes in Northwest Amazonia* (Cambridge: Cambridge University Press)

Hugh-Jones, S. (1979), *The Palm and the Pleiades: Initiation and Cosmology in Northwest Amazonia* (Cambridge: Cambridge University Press)

Lafitau, J. F. (1724), *Moeurs des sauvages Amériquains comparées aux moeurs des premiers temps* (Paris)

Leach, E. R. (1954), *Political Systems of Highland Burma: A Study of Kachin Social Structure* (London: G. Bell & Sons [later editions Athlone Press])

—— (1961), *Pul Eliya: A Village in Ceylon* (Cambridge: Cambridge University Press)

—— (1980), *L'Unité de l'homme et autres essais* (Paris: Gallimard)

Lévi-Strauss, C. (1949), *Les Structures élémentaires de la parenté* (Paris: PUF)

—— (1962), *La Pensée sauvage* (Paris: Plon)

—— (1964–71), *Mythologiques*, 4 vols (Paris: Plon)

—— (1968), *Structural Anthropology* (London: Allen Lane)

Lin Yueh-hwa (1948), *The Golden Wing: A Sociological Study of Chinese Familism* (London: Kegan Paul)

Linné, Sir C. (Linnaeus) (1735), *A General System of Nature* (various editions)

Locke, J. (1690), *An Essay concerning Human Understanding* (London)

Maine, H. S. (1861), *Ancient Law* (London: John Murray)

Maistre, J. de (1797), 'Considerations sur la France'

Malinowski, B. (1922), *Argonauts of the Western Pacific* (London: Routledge)

—— (1929), *The Sexual Life of Savages in North-Western Melanesia* (London: Routledge)

—— (1935), *Coral Gardens and their Magic*, 2 vols (London: Allen and Unwin)

'Mandeville' (C14), *The Travels of Sir John Mandeville*

Montaigne, M. de (1580), *Essais* (My quotations are taken from the Penguin Classics edition translated by J. M. Cohen)

More, H. (1653), *Conjectura Cabbalistica*

Morgan, L. H. (1871), *Systems of Consanguinity and Affinity of the Human Family*, Smithsonian Contributions to Knowledge No.

218 (Washington: Smithsonian Institution)

—— (1877), *Ancient Society* (New York: Henry Holt & Co.)

Murdock, G. P. (1949), *Social Structure* (New York: Macmillan)

Radcliffe-Brown, A. R. (1922) *The Andaman Islanders* (Cambridge: Cambridge University Press)

Radcliffe-Brown, A. R. and Daryll Forde (eds) (1950), *African Systems of Kinship and Marriage* (London: Oxford University Press)

Raglan, Lord (1964), *The Temple and the House* (New York: W. W. Norton)

Roberts, J. M. (1964), 'The Self Management of Cultures' in W. H. Goodenough (ed.), *Explorations in Cultural Anthropology* (New York: McGraw-Hill), pp. 433–54.

Schmitt, J.-C. (1979), *Le saint levrier: Guinefort, guerisseur d'enfants depuis le XIIIeme siècle* (Paris: Flammarion)

Schneider, D. M. (1968), *American Kinship: A Cultural Account* (Englewood Cliffs, N.J.: Prentice Hall Inc.)

—— (1976), 'Notes toward a Theory of Culture' in K. H. Basso and H. A. Selby (eds), *Meaning in Anthropology* (Albuquerque: University of New Mexico Press), pp. 197–220.

Sebeok, T. A. and Sebeok, J. U. (1980), *Speaking of Apes: A Critical Anthology of Two-Way Communication with Man* (New York: Plenum Publishing Corp.)

Turner, V. W. (1969), *The Ritual Process: Structure and Anti-Structure* (London: Routledge and Kegan Paul)

Tylor, E. B. (1871), *Primitive Culture*, 2 vols (London: John Murray)

—— (1889), 'On a method of investigating the development of institutions; applied to laws of marriage and descent', *The Journal of the Anthropological Institute*, Vol. xviii, pp. 245–74.

Tyson, Sir W. (1708), *Orang-outang, sive homo silvestris; or the anatomy of a pygmie*

Van Gennep, A. (1908), *Les Rites de Passage* (Paris)

Vico, G. (1744), *The New Science of Giambattista Vico*, (translated from the 3rd edition by T. G. Bergin and M. H. Fisch, Ithaca: Cornell University Press [1948])

Wilson, E. O. (1978), *On Human Nature* (Cambridge, Mass: Harvard University Press)

Wittfogel, K. A. (1957), *Oriental Despotism: A Comparative Study of Total Power* (New Haven: Yale University Press)

Yang, M. C. (1948), *A Chinese Village: Taitou, Shantung Province* (London: Kegan Paul)

Index

254 *Index*